Herp Help

LENNY FLANK, JR.

FEATURING PHOTOGRAPHS
BY
BILL LOVE

HOWELL
BOOK
HOUSE

For Mindy and Rich Does, who were there for me more times than I can remember. Thanks for everything.

Howell Book House
A Simon & Schuster Macmillan Company
1633 Broadway
New York, NY 10019

Macmillan Publishing books may be purchased for business or sales promotional use. For information write: Special Markets Department, Macmillan Publishing USA, 1633 Broadway, New York, NY 10019.

Macmillan is a registered trademark of Macmillan, Inc.

Library of Congress Cataloging-in-Publication Data
Flank, Lenny.
Herp help/Lenny Flank, Jr.; featuring photographs by Bill Love.
    p. cm.
    Includes index.
    ISBN: 0-87605-634-6
    1. Captive reptiles. 2. Captive amphibians. 3. Reptiles as pets.
    4. Amphibians as pets. I. Title.
SF515.F58 1998   97-46607
639.3'78--dc21   CIP

Manufactured in the United States

Book design by Nick Anderson

Contents

Acknowledgments

A number of people made this book possible. Thanks must go to the fine folks at Glades Herp, who provided many of the species for photographs as well as most of my own personal herp collection. Bill Love, one of the foremost herp photographers in the world, has done fine photographic work for this and other books. The staff at Howell Book House are a joy to work with (they even let me get away with missing several deadlines for this book). And thanks go to my parents, who didn't complain (much) about the zoo I kept in my bedroom all those years ago.

Preface

For most people, the words "reptile" and "amphibian" conjure up repulsive images of scaly, slimy creatures—apparitions of evil, such as the serpent of Genesis, or Kaa, the slithering villain of *The Jungle Book*. These are the people who rush hurriedly through the reptile house at the local zoo, or who would refuse to enter a patch of woods or tall grass if they had any inkling that a snake or lizard might be lurking within.

For some of us, however, the words "reptile" and "amphibian" conjure up images of fascinating creatures who are attractive in their very alien-ness—the staring unblinking eyes, the slow fluid movements, the dazzling array of shapes and colors. These people find interest in the lives of such creatures, their intricate predator-prey relationships, and their pivotal place in the web of life.

Those of you who always want to have a reptile or an amphibian nearby so you can admire its beauty and study its ways, this book was written for you.

When I first began collecting and studying reptiles and amphibians, some 15 years ago, there was virtually no reliable information to be found on keeping and caring for these creatures, and the only way to obtain a variety of herps was to capture them yourself. Today, however, herpetoculture (the keeping and raising of reptiles and amphibians in captivity) is one of the fastest-growing hobbies in the United States. Several million herps are bred in or imported into the United States each year—most as pets—and it is estimated that about seven percent of all families in the country—almost two million people—keep at least one reptile or amphibian as a pet. A number of magazines such as *Reptile and Amphibian, The Vivarium,* and *Reptiles Magazine,* cater to the herpetoculturalists and even Internet mail lists and newsgroups have become specialized sources for herpers to exchange information, advice, stories and sometimes specimens.

Despite this, however, there remains no good reference work for the beginning herpetoculturalist, one which provides an introduction to the biology and natural history of these unique animals as well as providing basic information on the care of a broad range of individual species.

This book was written to help fill that need. It presents a basic introduction to the lifestyles of reptiles and amphibians, and gives helpful advice on keeping and raising the most commonly available frogs, salamanders, turtles, lizards, and snakes. If this book encourages just one hobbyist into beginning a serious study of these fascinating animals, or if it awakens just one person to the need to protect and maintain these animals and the roles they play in nature, then it will have served its purpose.

Happy herping!

Introduction

Although reptiles and amphibians belong to two very different classes of vertebrate animals, modern science tends to join them together into one scientific discipline, called "herpetology." Collectively, reptiles and amphibians are usually referred to as "herpetofauna" or "herpetological specimens," a phrase which is nearly always shortened to "herps."

Amphibians belong to the class Amphibia, a name which comes from the Greek words for "two lives." The distinguishing characteristic of all amphibians is the two distinct stages in their life cycle. The eggs are laid in water and hatch into aquatic young known as "larvae." The familiar tadpole or polliwog is the larval stage of the group of amphibians known as Anura, which includes the frogs and toads. The group of amphibians known as Caudata, the salamanders, also have aquatic larvae. A third group of amphibians, the Caecelians, are not commonly encountered in the pet trade and are not widely studied. Very little is known about their habits or biology. Upon reaching maturity, all of these groups of amphibians leave the water and take up a terrestrial existence (although some members of all three groups remain aquatic even as adults).

In addition to the distinct aquatic and terrestrial stages in their life history, amphibians are also distinguished by a number of other factors. Nearly all amphibians have a very thin and delicate skin that they use for breathing (some of the salamanders have done away with lungs completely and depend solely on skin respiration). This skin is water-permeable and dries out quickly, and this fact is of paramount importance in the habits and lifestyles of all the amphibians. Adult amphibians are almost never found far from a permanent source of water, and all of them require damp humid surroundings to prevent their skins from dessicating and drying out.

The dependence upon water is most acute during reproduction. The eggs of all amphibians are coated with a jelly-like covering which helps to protect the developing embryo. This gelatinous coating, however, dries out quickly upon exposure to air, killing the young amphibian. For this reason, all amphibians must lay their eggs in damp wet places, and most species can only lay their eggs in a body of water. This requirement has placed severe restrictions on the ability of the amphibians to diversify into new environmental niches.

The reptiles belong to the vertebrate class Reptilia, which comes from the Latin word meaning "to crawl." There are five existing groups or orders of reptiles. The turtles and tortoises make up the order known as Chelonia. The snakes make up the suborder Serpentes, while the lizards are grouped into the suborder Sauria (because these two suborders are very closely related, they are combined into the order Squamata). A fourth order, known as Rhyncocephalia, or "beak-heads," is a very ancient group of reptiles with only one living member, the rare tuatara, a large lizard-like animal found near New Zealand. The fifth order of reptiles are the Amphisbaenids, which are little-known wormlike animals that live underground.

Reptiles are distinguished from amphibians by their thick scaly skin, which protects the animal from scratches and abrasions much more effectively than the thin delicate skin of amphibians. More importantly, the reptilian skin is waterproof and retains body moisture, freeing the animal from the necessity of remaining in a damp or wet place to avoid dessication. Because of their impervious skins, reptiles have been able to colonize a much wider variety of ecological niches than have amphibians, and in some ecological zones, such as deserts, reptiles are the dominant form of life.

Even more important to the success of the reptiles was the development of the amniote egg. Unlike the naked exposed egg of the amphibians, the reptile egg is surrounded by a hard protective shell, which protects the developing embryo and also traps fluids and moisture inside the egg, preventing it from drying out. In effect, the reptile has solved the problem of laying eggs on land by taking a tiny private pond along with it inside the egg shell, within which the embryo can develop in relative safety. The amniote egg, which first appeared over 200 million years ago, was the key to the success of the reptiles, and was also the trigger that first allowed the successful colonization of the land by the ancient vertebrates. Unlike the amphibians, who must go through a vulnerable aquatic larval stage before reaching maturity, the reptile hatches from its egg fully developed, as a miniature copy of its parents, ready to fend for itself.

Reptiles and amphibians have been spectacularly successful animals. Numerically, there are over three times as many living species of herps as there are warm-blooded mammals. In many ecological systems, the reptiles and amphibians are the dominant species. In the "large freshwater predator" niche, for instance, reptiles are virtually unchallenged. The crocodilians are the undisputed top of the food chain, and nearly every river system in tropical areas is prowled by crocodiles, alligators, or gavials. Other large aquatic predators include some of the monitor lizards, the large constrictor snakes like anacondas, and the big turtles such as snappers and softshells. By contrast, the only large mammal that regularly inhabits freshwater river systems is the hippopotamus, which is not a predator.

In the "small freshwater predator" niche, the mammals make a better showing, but herps still reign supreme. About 50 species of mammals make their living in freshwater ponds, streams and rivers— including otters, muskrats, and beavers. By contrast, over 1,250 species of reptile and amphibian inhabit this niche. The frogs are the masters of this habitat— almost 1,000 species of frogs can be found in freshwater environments. Some 100 species of newt and aquatic salamander prowl freshwater areas, and both frogs and newts are preyed on by the freshwater turtles. Aside from fishes, the reptiles and amphibians are by far the most numerous vertebrates to be found in any freshwater ecological system.

Herps also numerically dominate the "small terrestrial predator" niche. Over 6,000 species of reptile and amphibian can be found roaming terrestrial areas, in habitats ranging from cool northern boreal pine forests to steaming tropical rain forests. By contrast, the warm-blooded mammals can boast at best some 2,500 terrestrial species—most of which are not predators.

At present, mammals are able to dominate herps in only two environmental niches. The "marine predator" niche has barely been penetrated by reptiles (only the sea snakes and a handful of marine turtles regularly enter the seas), and no amphibians can be found in saltwater. The mammals are represented in this niche by the cetaceans (dolphins and whales), which are quite a successful group of animals.

Although the reptiles used to dominate the "large terrestrial animal" niche, since the end of the Mesozoic era the mammals have reigned supreme. Only the large constricting snakes, the giant tortoises, and the largest of the monitor lizards can claim membership in this ecological guild. The mammals, by contrast, make up nearly all of the 100 largest terrestrial animals. Most of the very large reptiles can survive only in remote island areas where mammalian competition is absent (the Komodo dragon and the Galapagos tortoise) or by remaining hidden and inconspicuous to potential mammalian predators (the large pythons).

In some particular terrestrial habitats, however, herps can outcompete the mammals. In desert areas, the reptilian waterproof skin and low need for food allows them to thrive in areas where mammals cannot survive for very long.

Ectothermy

Although amphibians and reptiles differ in many ways, one characteristic they both share is known as "ectothermy." Mammals and birds are said to be "warm-blooded," which means that they can maintain a high internal body temperature no matter what the outside temperature might be, by producing their own metabolic body heat. Reptiles and amphibians, on the other hand, are "ectothermic," which means that they cannot produce their own internal body heat, but are dependent upon outside sources of heat to maintain a high body temperature. Body temperature is an important factor for all organisms, because many biological processes depend upon enzymes and other chemicals that work well at some temperatures and not so well at others. In areas that are too cold, ectotherms cannot maintain a body temperature high enough to carry on their biological processes, and they will die. On the other hand, if the external temperature is too high, the reptile or amphibian has no means by which to cool itself (herps have no sweat glands and cannot lower their body temperature by perspiring like a mammal can) and will also die.

Thus, temperature control becomes a vital factor for any herp, as well as for any herp keeper. In general, amphibians can tolerate a lower range of body temperatures than reptiles. Each species, however, will have a preferred body temperature at which particular biological processes will function best. The actual preferred temperature will vary depending on the time of day, the specific activity that is required, and the size and age of the herp. Since the herp keeper has no way of knowing what temperature is preferred at any given moment, he must provide a range of temperatures and allow the herp to move from warmer to cooler areas ("thermoregulate") as it desires. For this reason, maintaining a proper temperature gradient, ranging from a "hot spot" for basking at one end of the cage to a cooler shaded spot at the other end, is a critical part of proper care of captive reptiles and amphibians.

Because reptiles and amphibians can inhabit a wide variety of ecological niches, from cool, temperate forests to dry, arid deserts to hot, humid, tropical jungles, each particular species will require its own specialized care. Here, then, is a look at the requirements for keeping and raising the most commonly available herps in captivity. Each species listing contains some interesting biological facts, as well as specialized information on housing, feeding and breeding. There is also a short "thumbnail" sketch giving information on the level of experience necessary to keep this species (from Novice to Intermediate to Advanced), the rough size one can expect from this species (from Small to Medium to Large to Extra Large) and a note on habitat.

PART I

Basic Care of Reptiles and Amphibians

The Essentials

CHAPTER 1

The Essentials

The essential elements of successful herp keeping include adequate housing and good nutrition. The following outlines the basic needs of all different kinds of herps.

Housing

The Terrestrial Setup

A terrestrial setup is a typical reptile or amphibian setup, and will serve for many of the species that are commonly kept in captivity. The basic housing unit is an ordinary glass aquarium. For most reptiles and amphibians, you will also need a securely locking lid. Snakes in particular are accomplished escape artists, but even salamanders, with their damp bodies, can adhere to the glass of an aquarium and make their way up and out. A number of locking-screen lids are commercially available to fit the common aquarium sizes.

Some very good accommodations for small- and medium-sized herps can also be made from the plastic boxes sold in department stores for storing sweaters and other clothing. These are made from one piece of clear or translucent plastic and have matching lids that snap into place. They come in a variety of sizes and require little modification. Airholes need to be added along the top, the bottom, and on all four sides of the box to provide ventilation.

The most functional substrate for terrestrial snakes, lizards and turtles is ordinary newspaper. This can be cut to size and placed in the cage, three or four layers thick, and can be quickly and easily cleaned simply by removing the old layers,

Stacked sweater boxes can be used to house terrestrial snakes.

throwing them away and replacing them with fresh sheets.

Shredded tree bark, aspen wood chips (not wood shavings), cocoa bean shells, and ground-up corn cobs are all commercially available for use as cage substrates, and all work well.

Ordinary aquarium gravel is a workable substrate, but it's not very absorbent and will be difficult to keep clean unless it is either replaced often or periodically removed, rinsed and dried. Desert animals can be kept on aquarium gravel or on several inches of clean sand.

Terrestrial amphibians, of course, cannot tolerate these dry substrates, and will need a damp material in their cages. Shredded tree bark will hold a lot of water and stay moist, but the best substrate for salamanders and terrestrial frogs is a thick layer of moss with a few leafs and pieces of bark scattered on top for hiding places. This substrate will have to be misted every day.

Amphibians require somewhat cool temperatures and will not require any sources of supplemental heat. Most temperate species of reptile will also do well at ordinary room temperatures, as long as they are provided with a localized "hot spot" for basking and a source of unfiltered unltraviolet light. A suitable basking spot can be produced by focusing an ordinary light bulb in a reflector hood onto a rock or tree branch inside the cage. This basking light should be located outside the tank, at one corner, where the reptile cannot reach it.

This walk-in terrestrial cage is both functional and beautiful.

If it becomes necessary to provide supplemental heat for tropical species, small undertank heating pads are commercially available that stick onto the underside of the cage. The electric "hot rocks" or "sizzle stones" that are widely available in pet shops should not be used in any reptile's cage.

The Aquatic Setup

An aquatic setup is the easiest habitat to duplicate but is only suitable for a small number of captive herps. All that is needed is an ordinary tropical fish aquarium of the appropriate size with several inches of clean water. No land area is needed. If tap water is to be used, it should be allowed to stand overnight to allow the chlorine to dissipate before any animals are introduced.

No substrate is necessary—it will only become fouled with wastes and food and will necessitate frequent cleaning. Some turtles (musk and mud turtles) will need an underwater cave where they can hide during the day. This can be created by piling up natural rocks and cementing them together with aquarium sealer so they cannot be dislodged (a turtle may drown if it becomes trapped under a rockfall).

For large messy animals such as turtles, feeding should take place in a separate smaller tank, to avoid messes caused by uneaten food. If it is necessary to feed the animal in its home tank (snappers, for example, are difficult to move for feeding), a large powerful filter system should be set up to keep the water clear.

Animals from temperate areas will do well at ordinary room temperatures. Tropical animals, however, will need heated water. This is best provided using electric heaters commonly available for tropical fish tanks. These must be screened off by a pile of rocks to prevent the animals from knocking them around and breaking them. Or, if an outside power filter is being used, the heater can be placed in the filter, allowing heated water to run back into the aquarium.

The aquatic setup is suitable for keeping snappers, softshells, mud and musk turtles and african clawed frogs.

The Semi-Aquatic Setup

A semi-aquatic setup is a combination of the above two. It is suitable for most turtles, newts, many frogs and a few snakes. The basic concept is to have half of the tank set up as a terrestrial area and half as an aquatic area.

One way to do this is to place a large pile of rocks in one half of the tank which protrude above the surface of the water. To protect the delicate plastrons of turtles and the skin of amphibians, these should be covered with a thick layer of leaf litter or moss. The dry area should

A semi-aquatic setup can be quite elaborate—but the essence is to provide both dry land and water.

rise gently out of the water, to enable animals to climb into or out of the water easily.

Another option is to place a glass or plastic divider across the tank, which extends about halfway up the side of the aquarium. One side of the tank is then filled with water, and the other is filled with dry substrate and landscaped as a terrestrial tank. A flat rock or piece of driftwood must be postioned across the partition to provide a ramp for easy access. The basking light should be set up on the dry area of the tank, and a filter should be placed in the aquatic portion.

The Arboreal Setup

An arboreal setup is necessary for keeping specialized tree climbers, such as many of the boids, some of the rat snakes, the Cuban anoles and the tree frogs.

Arboreal cages must be tall with plenty of space for climbing. The "show" or "tall" style of aquarium is best for this purpose. The tall "hexagonal" tanks are also suited for arboreal species, but unfortunately, no locking-screen lids are commercially available for these tanks.

Climbing branches for arboreal species must be strong and sturdy enough to support the weight of the animal without breaking and long enough to provide ample climbing space. Tree branches obtained from outdoors are safe, provided they are properly disinfected by soaking them overnight in a weak solution of bleach water. Rinse these thoroughly with plain water before placing them in the cage. Resinous woods such as pine or spruce should be avoided.

The substrate and heating for an arboreal tank can be set up in the same manner as for a terrestrial cage.

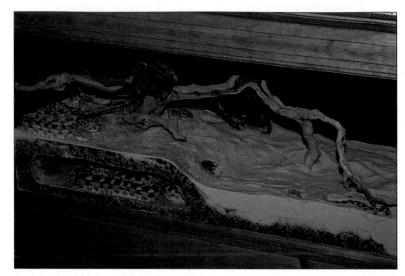

An unusual and fun accomodation for burrowers is to provide a subterranean lair complete with a view hole.

The Burrowers Setup

Burrowing herps, such as rosy boas, some of the mole salamanders, horned frogs and the sandfish or sand skinks, will require a substrate suitable to their habits.

Burrowing amphibians such as salamanders or large frogs require thick damp substrates. Soil and moss substrates work well and are not difficult to set up. Line the bottom of the tank with an inch or two of pea gravel for drainage. Cover this with a thin layer of activated charcoal (to control odors and to disinfect the substrate).

Then add two or three inches of clean potting soil. A layer of thick moss or deep leaf litter goes on top of this. Finally, a number of rocks or flat pieces of bark are arranged to form hiding spots. The tank must be misted daily to keep it damp.

Desert burrowers such as rosy boas or skinks can be kept in several inches of clean playground sand. This should be changed when it gets fouled. The heating and lighting requirements for such a setup are the same as those for a terrestrial tank.

Many of the boids, like this emerald tree boa, need sturdy branches to climb.

Selecting Cage Mates

In general, herps are not social animals and interact very little with each other or other species. Most reptiles and amphibians therefore do best if they are housed alone. A few species are fiercely territorial and will not tolerate the presence of another member of its own species. Other species are aggressive and will attack and eat anything else in their tank. Only a few species, such as green anoles and some of the turtles, regularly share their living space with others.

It may be possible to house several species from the same geographic region and habitat together in one very large tank. Garter and ribbon snakes, for example, will often share a tank happily together, as will most of the semi-aquatic frogs and semi-aquatic turtles. Mixing species from different habitats, however, should be avoided, as it will be impossible to meet the differing environmental needs of these animals in one tank. Inevitably, one (or perhaps both) species will weaken and die. Also, housing species from different geographic regions together in one tank should be avoided because each may be carrying live exotic pathogens to which the others will have no natural immunity.

Feeding

Plant Foods

Only a few of the living reptiles are herbivorous. These include the iguanas, some of the skinks and many of the terrestrial tortoises. The basic diet consists of leafy green vegetables such as endive, collard greens, mustard greens, dandelion leaves, carrot tops and mulberry leaves. Limited amounts of ripe fruit such as melons, squash, berries and tropical fruits can also be offered. Lettuce should be avoided, as it contains mostly water and cellulose and has no nutritional value.

Herbivorous animals cannot obtain as much food value from their diet as carnivores do, and thus must eat more often. Most herbivorous reptiles should be fed every day or two.

Insect Foods

Most of the lizards and nearly all of the frogs and toads are "bug crunchers." High in protein and fat, insects are an excellent food source. Insectivorous herps should be fed often enough that there are always a few insects in the tank.

The most common insect food is crickets, which are commercially available from large cricket farms. To ensure the highest food value, crickets must be "gut-loaded" before they are fed to reptiles or amphibians. This is done by feeding several meals to the crickets before they are themselves used as food. Although crickets will eat just about anything, the best food for them consists of high-protein fare like dry dog food or commercial tropical fish flakes. An amount of vegetable food such as potato or apple should also be provided.

Before being fed to lizards or other reptiles, crickets should be lightly dusted with calcium and vitamin powder.

Other insect foods are also available for captive reptiles and amphibians. The so-called "mealworms" are actually the immature larvae of a small beetle. Mealworms are acceptable as an occasional treat, but should not form the bulk of the diet because their hard chitinous outer skins are indigestible and can clog up a herp's intestines.

Fruit flies are also widely available, and they make good foods for small frogs and some salamanders. A variety of fruit fly known as "vestigial" lacks wings and cannot fly, which makes it a good food source. Wild fruit flies can be captured by setting a piece of ripe banana in a jar and placing this near a window. Materials for raising colonies of these insects can be obtained from biological supply houses.

Recently, wingless house flies have become commercially available, and these are good food resources for frogs and small lizards. Like all insect food, house flies should be gut-loaded before being used as herp food.

Many reptile keepers collect their own insect food from the wild, capturing butterflies, beetles, flies and other insects with nets or traps. This practice has the advantage of providing a variety of prey animals, which helps to ensure a balanced diet. If you capture wild foods for your herps, make sure they come from an area that has not been sprayed or treated with insecticides.

The tusked chameleon is adept at capturing its insect diet.

Invertebrate Foods

Earthworms, slugs and other invertebrates form the diet of several species of reptile and amphibian, such as garter snakes, many toads and most of the salamanders and newts. Such invertebrates can be collected from the wild or obtained at pet stores or bait shops.

Small aquatic or semi-aquatic herps will thrive on a diet of blood worms or tubifex worms, which are available at tropical fish shops. Brine shrimp can also be fed to aquatic herps. These are small marine crustaceans, the dried eggs of which are commonly sold in novelty stores as "sea monkeys." These should be rinsed thoroughly in fresh water to remove the excess salt before being introduced to the herp tank.

Terrestrial animals, such as large salamanders or snakes, can be fed ordinary earthworms or "nightcrawlers." These can be captured during rainy nights using a flashlight. They can also be purchased in bait shops.

Fish

Fish form the staple diet of the aquatic turtles, such as snappers and softshells. Garter, ribbon and water snakes also include fish in their diet.

Small herps can be fed ordinary goldfish. The fish should be fed several meals using a good quality tropical fish food before being offered to the herps. Some turtles, such as musk or mud turtles, are not fast enough to catch live goldfish—in these cases, the fish should be stunned or killed before being introduced to the tank. Fish-eating snakes can be fed simply by placing several goldfish in the tank's water bowl. The snakes will capture and swallow them.

Larger herps can be fed frozen fish such as smelts. If possible, these should be obtained intact, with the head and guts still present. The fish are thoroughly thawed in warm water before being offered to the reptile on tongs or forceps.

Rodent Foods

Most snakes, all of the large predatory lizards, and some of the largest frogs and toads will live happily on a diet of rodents. Whole mice, which includes the viscera and stomach contents, are a nutritionally complete diet for all herps that will eat them. No other vitamin supplements or dietary additions are needed.

Large toads and frogs, such as the giant toad and the horned frogs, can be fed live juvenile mice—known as "pinkies" or "fuzzies." These will be swallowed live. Very large salamanders, such as tiger salamanders, will also eat pinkies.

Monitors, tegus and snakes should be fed pre-killed mice, in order to avoid accidental bites and injuries caused by live prey. Frozen mice and other rodents can be bulk-ordered and should be individually and thoroughly thawed for use as food. Rodents should be offered on tongs or forceps.

The large boids need larger prey and can be offered frozen-and-thawed foods, such as large rats, rabbits or chickens.

Prepared Foods

A number of commercially prepared foods are now available for captive reptiles and amphibians. These foods offer no real advantages over unprocessed food animals—and are more expensive—but may be the only choice for herpers who live in urban areas.

Snake "sausages" are made from ground-up mice. They are more expensive than pre-killed mice, and many snakes will refuse to eat them. However, they offer an alternative to snake keepers who do not wish to feed intact rodents to their herps.

Monitors and tegus can be fed a commercial canned food made from horse meat, eggs and other additives. If a pinch of calcium and vitamin powder is added to every other meal, these foods make a good staple diet. Usually, these large lizards will also eat ordinary canned dog food; this should be a low-fat variety, such as chicken or fish, with a low ash content.

Canned turtle and tortoise foods are also available. These contain a mixture of vegetables and fruits. A similar canned food is available for iguanas. This should be supplemented with calcium powder and fresh vegetables and fruits. Dry iguana foods are also sometimes seen—these should be mixed sparingly with fresh greens and fruits.

PART II

Amphibians

Frogs and Toads · Salamanders

CHAPTER 2

Frogs and Toads

All frogs and toads are members of the Anura family of amphibians, which means "no tails." In popular usage, the term "frog" refers to those anurans that live near water and have smooth moist skin and large rear legs for leaping, while "toads" live far from water and have dry warty skin and short rear legs. To a biologist, however, the term "toad" is reserved solely for members of the families bufonids (the "true toads") and pelobatids (the "spadefoot toads").

There are about 2,700 species of frogs and toads. They are a very diverse group, geographically ranging from the equatorial tropics to the Arctic circle and living in habitats from rain forests to arid deserts.

Ranids

The "true frogs," this family contains most of the familiar pond frogs, including the bullfrog, pickerel frog and leopard frog. It also includes species such as the South African bullfrog. About 600 members of this family are found throughout the world. In Africa they are the dominant frog family. Although the ranid family contains several genera, all of the ranids in the United States belong to the large genus *Rana.*

Bullfrogs are part of the ranid family (albino bullfrog).

Bufonids

The bufonids family of "true toads" contains the common American toad as well as the green toad and giant toad. There are about 300 species of true toad found virtually throughout the world. (There are no toads in Madagascar, and the only toad found in Australia, the cane toad or giant toad, was introduced recently by man).

The true toads are distinguished from other anurans by the large paratoid glands on the back of their neck, which secrete a poison called bufotoxin to protect the animal from predators. The toxin oozes from pores in the paratoid gland whenever the toad is alarmed. The toxin is harmless to humans and, contrary to popular belief, does not produce warts.

Brachycephalids

This "short-headed toads" family consists of just two species of small forest toads from Brazil. They are sometimes included in the bufonid family.

Hylids

There are about 600 species of tree frogs found throughout the world, on virtually every continent but Antarctica. The largest genus in the family, *Hyla,* is not found in Australia. In the tropical rain forests in Latin America, the tree frogs are the dominant anuran family.

Tree frogs are small and highly specialized for an arboreal existence. Many species spend their whole lives in trees and never descend to the ground, not even to lay eggs.

Microhylids

This large "narrowmouth toads" family is found in Africa, Madagascar, Latin America, Asia and Australasia. Three species are found in the United States. They are burrowing frogs that only emerge after rains.

Dendrobatids

The poison arrow frogs comprise a large and varied family, consisting of some 116 species found in Latin America. Most species are very small in size, but their diurnal habits and their vivid colors make them conspicuous. Two genera,

Tree frogs are highly specialized for an arboreal life (*Boophi* sp. tree frog, Madagascar).

Dendrobates and *Phyllobates,* have powerful toxins in their skin and bright warning colors. The third genus, *Colostethus,* lack toxins and are dull brown in color.

Discoglossids

A rather primitive family of eleven species, which includes the Oriental fire bellied toad and the European midwife toad. The discoglossids lack an extendable tongue and capture their food by stuffing it into their mouths with their front limbs. Most live in or near water. The family ranges from Europe to North Africa with an isolated group in the Phillipine Islands.

The midwife toad is famous for its parental care of the eggs, which are carried by the male on his back until they hatch and produce tadpoles.

Pelobatids

Although they resemble the true toads, the spadefoot toads are distinguished by the horny protrusions on their rear feet, which they use for digging and burrowing. They also lack paratoid glands. Members of the family can be found in Europe, Asia, northern Africa and North America. The six species found in the United States are all from the same genus.

Spadefoots spend most of their time in underground chambers, emerging after heavy showers to breed.

Pipids

Consisting of the Surinam toad and its relatives, this aquatic family includes about twenty-six species found in the northern part of Latin America and sub-Saharan Africa. One species, the African clawed frog, has been established in the United States. Among frogs, they have the unusual characteristic of lacking tongues.

Rhinophrynids

This family contains only one living species, the Mexican burrowing toad. This unusual frog is found in Mexico and southern Texas and spends most of its time in an underground burrow, emerging briefly after heavy rains.

The Oriental fire bellied toad lacks an extendable tongue.

Ascaphids

Here's another single-species family, which contains only the tailed frog of the western United States. Males of this species have a protruding "tail" (actually the everted cloaca) which they use as a copulatory organ during breeding. Some taxonomists have argued in favor of classifying the tailed frog together with some unusual frogs of the *Leiopelma* genus in New Zealand.

Leptodactylids

This large group, containing about 500 species, is found largely in rainforests and its members are usually referred to as tropical frogs. Species can be found in Latin America, Australasia and the southern United States.

The leptodactylids vary widely in habits. Some are arboreal, some are burrowers and most are terrestrial. A few lay eggs on land which undergo metamorphosis and hatch as fully formed froglets. One species from Puerto Rico is unusual in retaining the eggs in its cloaca and giving birth to living froglets.

Ceratophrytids

The horned frogs and their relatives include nine species, all found in Latin America. Some taxonomists lump this group together with the leptodactylids.

This tiny Argentine horned frog holds on tight when it wants to.

Myobatrachids

This large family, containing some 106 species, is found exclusively in Australia. They are varied in habitat and lifestyle. The genus *Neobatrachus* is desert-dwelling, while the genus *Limnodynastes* prefers damp habitats. The most unusual genus is *Rheobatrachus,* which contains two species (one is probably now extinct) of stomach-brooders.

Rhinodermatids

There are only two species in this mouthbreeding frogs family, both found in Argentina and Chile. The males carry the eggs in their vocal sacs, where they hatch and develop into froglets.

Rhacophorids

In many ways, this large family of frogs found in Africa and Asia parallel the habits of the American hylids. Most are arboreal. A few species in the *Rhacophorus* genus have extensive webbing between their toes which they can use as a parachute to glide from tree to tree, earning them the name "flying frogs."

Hyperoliids

The reed frogs and sedge frogs number around 170 species in Africa and Madagascar. Most climb well and have adhesive toe pads. A few, the running frogs, are terrestrial.

Heleophrynids

The small ghost frogs family consist of three species of South African frogs. These live in swift streams and have adhesive pads on their toes to help them cling to wet rocks.

Pelotydids

This is a small family with just two species, known as parsley frogs. They are found in France and Spain.

Pseudids

This family is made up of four species from Latin America. The best-known species is the paradox frog, which has tadpoles over three times the size of the metamorphosed adult frog.

Centrolenids

The glass frogs contain about sixty-five species found exclusively in Latin America. The skin is extremely thin and transparent, allowing the internal organs to be seen.

Natural History

The earliest natural history of the anurans is largely unknown, because their delicate bones are only rarely fossilized. It is believed that they developed from the labrynthodont amphibians which flourished in the Carboniferous period approximately 300 million years ago. Another branch of the labrynthodonts went on to produce the salamanders, while a third branch led to the cotylosaur "stem reptiles," from which modern snakes, lizards and turtles are descended.

The earliest recognizable frogs appear in the Jurassic period, about 180 million years ago. These four-inch skeletons, known as *Triadobatrachus,* have been found in Madagascar.

In many characteristics, the *Triadobatrachus* fossil is intermediate between the modern frogs and their labrynthodont ancestors. The skull is very froglike, with a large sphenethmoid bone, fused frontal and parietal bones (although these are longer than they are in any modern frog) and large open orbital sockets. The ilium is much longer than in the earlier labrynthodonts but not as long as it is in modern frogs. The skull structure and elongated ilium, along with the large back legs and the lack of ribs, immediately mark *Triadobatrachus* as a very primitive frog.

Many of these features, however, are only poorly developed in *Triadobatrachus* and seem to be in the process of evolving towards the modern anuran condition. The ilium in *Triadobatrachus* lacks a strong articulation with the vertebral column, unlike modern frogs. The urostyle is also absent, and *Triadobatrachus* has a short tail, something no modern frog has. The spine, though somewhat shorter than in labrynthodonts, is still almost twice as long as any modern frog, and the rear legs are proportionately still very small, though somewhat larger than the front legs. The tibia and fibula bones in the lower leg are unfused and separate, making it probable that *Triadobatrachus* was not a very efficient leaper. The bones of the pectoral girdle are relatively small and light, unlike the heavy pectoral bones of the modern frogs, which are built to withstand the enormous jarring forces encountered upon landing after a long leap.

Thus, *Triadobatrachus,* far from exhibiting the typical anuran body structure, instead seems to possess a very primitive version of it and still retains several of the characteristics of its labrynthodont ancestors. The tail vertebrae, the lack of a urostyle, the free ilium and the unfused tibia and fibula are all characteristics possessed by the labrynthodonts but not possessed by any other frog species, living or extinct. On the other hand, the large spenethmoid, the elongated ilium, the lack of ribs and the large flat skull structure are typical of frogs but not of labrynthodont amphibians. *Triadobatrachus* thus seems to combine traits from two very different groups of animals and can only be viewed as an evolutionary transition between these two groups.

Another fossil frog, discovered in Arizona and called *Prosalirus bitis,* was uncovered in 1985, and dates from roughly the same time as *Triadobatrachus.* Like *Triadobatrachus, Prosalirus* did not have greatly enlarged legs but possessed the typical three-pronged pelvic structure. Unlike *Triadobatrachus, Prosalirus* had already lost nearly all of its tail. Without further fossil discoveries, it is impossible to tell whether *Triadobatrachus* or *Prosalirus* was the ultimate ancestor of modern frogs (or indeed whether these represent two distinct lineages within modern frogs). But it does demonstrate that already in the Triassic period, the frogs had diversified with the more primitive *Triadobatrachus* living alongside the more "modern" *Prosalirus,* just as the relatively primitive discoglossid frogs still live alongside the more advanced ranids.

Some of the best-preserved "modern" frog fossils are found in Wyoming and date to the Miocene period. These skeletons, named *Paleobatrachus* ("ancient frog") have been dated to 15 million years ago. Even the fossilized tadpoles of this extinct frog have been found.

Biology and Anatomy

Frogs and toads are readily recognized by their large heads, short squat bodies and their long muscular back legs. Like all herps, frogs and toads are ectothermic and cannot produce their own body heat—they are dependent upon

outside sources to maintain their body temperatures. As a group, however, frogs and toads can tolerate much cooler temperatures than reptiles. While most reptiles need temperatures in the high 70s, frogs can live happily in temperatures as low as the 60s. Because of their greater temperature tolerance, frogs and toads are distributed much more widely than are reptiles. In temperate areas, they are capable of hibernating for long periods, existing solely on their stored food reserves and the oxygen that diffuses through their thin skins.

Frogs, like all amphibians, are not amniotes and cannot lay shelled eggs. For this reason, they are dependent upon water for reproduction, and even the desert spadefoot toads can only reproduce in standing water.

Eyes

Frogs are very nearsighted and have to make an effort to focus their eyes on faraway objects. Unlike

most vertebrates, which focus their eyes by changing the shape of the lens, frogs and toads must focus by moving the whole lens back and forth.

Frogs have a number of reflexes "hard-wired" into their nervous systems. They will automatically snap at any small erratically moving object (a reflex known as the "bug detector") or any long object that moves (the "worm detector"). They will also dive for cover if a large shadow passes over them (a reflex that protects against predators). In all of these reflexes, the nerve signal travels directly to the spinal cord and back; the brain is not involved in any of these actions.

Skull

Frogs have very large skulls in proportion to their body size, but they have many air spaces and are very light. Frog teeth are simple, cone-shaped and attached to the rim of the jawbones as well as the bones in the roof of the mouth. In frogs, the teeth are usually absent from the lower jaw, while most toads have no teeth on either jawbone.

A frog's eyes float freely in the skull and are not surrounded by bony sockets. As a result, the eyeballs are free to bulge down into the throat through the roof of the mouth, where they are used to help push food into the stomach. Frogs thus use their eyes to help them swallow.

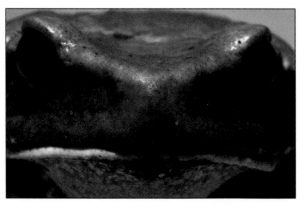

Frogs and toads must focus their eyes by moving the whole lens back and forth.

Ears

Frogs have well-developed ears and can hear quite well. The eardrum on most frogs and toads is clearly visible as a large round object on the side of the head. The amphibians were the first vertebrates to have a true voice; they sing by pushing air over the vocal cords and using the vocal sacs as a resonator.

Frogs hear some frequencies much better than others—usually those frequencies at which they call. Thus, although they can hear the calls of their own species from several miles away, frogs and toads may be literally deaf to the mating calls of other species.

Skin

Frog skin is very loosely connected to the body and secretes a large amount of mucus that acts as a lubricant in water and as a moisturizer on land. These mucus glands are scattered all over the frog's body. In addition, all frogs and toads secrete toxic chemicals in their skin to defend against predators. In toads, these are concentrated in the paratoid glands behind the eye; in most frogs, they are concentrated in the dorso-lateral folds along the back. In some species, the toxin is very mild; the poison arrow frogs, on the other hand, have some of the strongest biological toxins known to science.

Like all herps, frogs must periodically shed their skin in order to grow. A well-fed frog may shed his skin as often as every other day. Some tree frogs shed their skin virtually every night. In all frogs, the skin peels off in patches and is usually eaten.

Contrary to myth, touching frogs and toads cannot cause warts.

Pelvic Girdle

The pelvic girdles of frogs and toads have been heavily modified to conform to the leaping mode of locomotion, and this modification took place very early in frog evolution. The earliest known frogs, from the Mesozoic era, have the typical anuran pelvic structure. The bones of the pelvis are elongated and reinforced, and demonstrate a three-pronged structure that is resistant to bending and breaking. The spine is also short and lacks ribs. These modifications allow the spine to absorb and withstand the tremendous force generated by the powerful leg muscles whenever the frog leaps.

Cloaca

The cloaca is the opening shared by the frog's digestive, urinary and reproductive tracts. Unlike the more terrestrial reptiles, frogs and toads excrete their nitrogen wastes as water-soluble urea, rather than as dry uric acid crystals. This water loss is made up by absorbing moisture through the water-permeable skin.

Frogs also differ from reptiles in practicing external fertilization, in which the sperm are shed over the eggs after they are laid, rather than being introduced directly into the female's cloaca. Frogs and toads are thus completely dependent upon water for their ability to reproduce.

Tongue

The frog's tongue is its primary tool for obtaining food. Usually quite long, the tongue is attached at the front of the mouth but is free at the back, thus allowing it to be flipped out and extended for some distance. The end of the frog's tongue is coated with a sticky mucus which is used to entrap insects and other prey.

In some families of frogs, however—particularly frogs that are aquatic—the tongue is flat and round and cannot be extended from the mouth. These frogs must capture prey by pouncing on it with their open mouths. Most frogs and toads use their front feet to help stuff food into their mouths.

Heart

Like nearly all herps, frogs and toads have three-chambered hearts which allow the oxygenated blood returning from the lungs to become mixed with the unoxygenated blood returning from the body. Because the frog has such low oxygen requirements, this inefficient system works fairly well. However, it leaves the frog with little endurance. Because they tire quickly and cannot leap very far to escape predators, most frogs spend their whole lives within leaping distance of the water, where they can retreat and hide whenever danger threatens.

Stomach

The frog stomach is very elastic and can expand in size several times to hold large numbers of insect prey. In addition, its elastic qualities allow some frogs, such as the African bullfrog or the horned frog, to swallow such large prey as mice, birds and other frogs, even if the prey is almost as big as the predator.

In the now-extinct *Rheobatrachus* group, the stomach had an even more unusual use. In this family, the female swallowed her eggs as they were fertilized, and they hatched and developed into tadpoles in the stomach. After they completed their metamorphosis, they were regurgitated as froglets.

Toes

The toes of certain frogs, particularly the members of the tree frog family, have unique pads which aid them in climbing. The toe pads of a tree frog contain thousands of tiny wedge-shaped projections which grasp the small irregularities of surfaces, thus allowing them to grip walls and branches. In addition, the toe pads secrete a sticky

A tree frog's toe pads allow them to get a good grip on walls and branches.

mucus which acts like glue and forms a suction effect, allowing tree frogs to climb even such smooth surfaces as the glass sides of their terrarium. If it falls, a tree frog can cling to a tree branch even if just a single toe touches it.

Diseases
Red Leg

The disease most commonly found among captive frogs and toads is an infection by the bacteria *Aeromonas hydrophila,* which produces a condition known as "red leg." The symptoms include listless and lethargic behavior, and red irritated patches on the skin, produced by subcutaneous bursting of the blood vessels. These red patches are most clearly visible on the thin pale skin at the inside of the thighs, hence the name "red leg."

The condition is usually brought about by stresses such as overcrowding, poor diet or inadequate sanitation. The disease is highly contagious and spreads quickly. Untreated outbreaks can wipe out an entire colony of frogs. Treatment consists of disinfecting the tank with a weak solution of bleach, providing proper diet and environmental conditions, and administering tetracycline or some other antibiotic.

The best prevention is to avoid overcrowding and stressing your frogs, provide a balanced diet and try not to handle your frogs

A frog's skin is delicate (pig frog).

roughly. Torn or broken skin provides easy access for the bacteria. Using slightly medicated water will also help control the bacteria population and reduce the chances of infection. Note that Betadine, a common disinfectant and antibiotic used for reptiles, is toxic to amphibians. Other chemicals that are lethal to amphibians include bleach and hydrogen peroxide.

Wounds

Frog skin is delicate and easily injured. Small breaks in the skin can attract fungal spores which invade the body and produce swelling and injury. The frog or toad may have white cottony tufts at the site.

Treatment consists of submerging the frog in a weak Bactine or iodine solution several times a day until the infection is cleared up.

Species Descriptions

African Clawed Frog (Xenopus laevis)

Level: Novice
Size: Medium
Habitat: Tropical, Aquatic

Biology

African clawed frogs are entirely aquatic and virtually never leave the water. Although most of the frogs sold are juveniles, they grow quickly and can reach a length of six inches within a few years. Although native to the tropical parts of Africa, they have been widely introduced and used as lab animals.

For a time, the most reliable human pregnancy test utilized female African clawed frogs—the frogs would be injected with human urine, and if the hormones associated with pregnancy were present, the female frog would be induced to lay eggs.

Because they can tolerate a wide range of environmental conditions and because they will eat native species of fish, several states have outlawed the importation of African clawed frogs for fear that they will become established. Breeding populations already exist in Florida, California and other states.

Housing

African clawed frogs are completely aquatic and do not require any land area in their tanks. They prefer a gravel substrate with a number of rock piles for hiding, but if necessary, they can live happily in a bare tank with seven or eight inches of water. The water should be deep enough for the frogs to swim freely without touching bottom. Clawed frogs can tolerate brackish water much better than most other amphibians.

The frogs will spend most of the day sleeping at the bottom of the tank, waking at night to hang motionless at the water surface waiting for prey to happen by. Since they will often jump out of the tank accidentally, a tight-fitting lid is a necessity. No heater or aeration is required, but the water should be kept at normal room temperatures throughout the winter.

Feeding

African clawed frogs have no extendable tongue and use their large front feet to help stuff food into their mouths. The eyes are small and weak, and the frogs depend largely on their acute sense of smell to locate food. They are also very sensitive to vibrations in the water.

They will eat virtually any aquatic creature they can fit in their mouths, including insects, worms and small fish. If well fed, they can grow rapidly.

Breeding

Most captive breeders of African clawed frogs take advantage of extracted hormones which are injected into the pair to induce breeding and egg-laying. In the wild, they breed at the beginning of the tropical rainy season. To simulate these conditions in captivity, the water level in the tank should be suddenly increased, accompanied by a sharp drop in water temperature. Female African clawed frogs are much larger than their male counterparts, and also exhibit several small flaps of skin just in front of the cloaca.

The eggs are laid singly on the bottom of the tank. In rare instances, the adults will eat the newly laid eggs, and to prevent this, the eggs are often removed to another tank for incubation. Unlike most frog tadpoles, African clawed frog larvae are filter feeders and take up a characteristic head-down position at the surface and use their tiny tails to beat water into their mouths for feeding. Captive tadpoles can be fed on liquefied fish food.

American Toad
(Bufo americanus)

Level: Novice
Size: Small
Habitat: Temperate, Terrestrial/Burrower

Biology

The familiar American toad has a dry warty skin that retains water well, enabling it to wander far from water. Toads have good vision and can sense movement at quite a distance, but because of their squat heads, they cannot see anything closer than two or three inches from them. Toads have no teeth on their jaws, although they have a few teeth on the roof of their mouth.

Their primary defense is the milky toxin secreted by the large paratoid glands behind the eyes. This mild toxin cannot produce warts but can cause irritation if it enters the eyes. As a secondary defense, most toads will void the contents of their bladder if they are picked up. In captivity, they soon lose this habit.

Toads have lived up to thirty-one years in captivity and display a rather high intelligence for an amphibian. They can be taught to run a maze and can even remember the correct path for several weeks afterwards.

Housing

American toads can be housed in a typical woodland terrarium with a substrate of leaf litter or moss and several hiding places in the form of rocks or pieces of bark. They are not very active animals and in the wild, may live their whole lives in an area of less than 100 square feet. Although they can tolerate drier conditions than most amphibians, their cage should still be misted daily.

Toads cannot drink water but enjoy soaking themselves in a shallow water pan, absorbing moisture through the thin skin on their bellies and feet. They also like to dig and will often bury themselves in a patch of clean dirt or sand. They will normally bury themselves in this manner to hibernate through the winter, but can be kept active if the temperature is maintained in the 70s.

The American toad is similar in appearance and range to the Fowler's toad, which is sometimes sold as a "common toad." The Fowler's species is cared for in the same manner and can be kept in the same cage.

Feeding

American toads have huge appetites and will stuff themselves full at every opportunity. Insects of all sorts will be taken, including crickets, beetles, flies and grasshoppers. Toads are also fond of earthworms, which they will stuff into their mouths using their front feet, seizing one end and swallowing the worm like a piece of spaghetti. Three or four large insects a day is a sufficient diet for adults, supplemented with worms every few days.

Breeding

American toads are spring breeders and gather in shallow ponds by the dozens to mate. Toads can hear each other's mating calls at distances up to half a mile. During this time, male toads will frantically grasp at anything remotely toad-like, including rocks, boots and shoes, and even each other. If a male accidentally grasps another male, he is warned away by a specific "release call."

After amplexus, up to 12,000 eggs are laid among the vegetation. Unlike the eggs of frogs, which are laid in loose jelly-like masses, most toads lay their eggs in long tubes or strings. The eggs hatch into tiny black tadpoles after about a week. The metamorphosis process takes about two months, and the toadlets will usually emerge from the water during a warm rainy night. The toadlets reach sexual maturity in approximately two or three years.

Toad tadpoles are very sensitive to water conditions and will die or develop abnormally if the water becomes too acidic.

American toads will often hybridize with the similar Fowler's toad, *Bufo woodehousei fowleri,* which shares most of their range.

Bullfrog
(Rana catesbeiana)

Level: Novice
Size: Medium
Habitat: Temperate, Semi-Aquatic

Biology

At a length of eight inches and a weight of four pounds, the bullfrog is the largest frog in North America and one of the largest in the world. Captive bullfrogs have lived up to sixteen years.

The bullfrog is widely used as a laboratory animal, and several tadpoles and adult frogs were shot into orbit as part of the early American space program. Although they are native to the eastern part of the United States, some countries have attempted to farm bullfrogs as food sources, and they have been introduced into Cuba, Hawaii and Taiwan for this purpose. Escapees have established breeding populations in these areas. The bullfrog has also been widely introduced to the western United States, where it has eliminated or endangered a number of native species including the Vegas Valley leopard frog, which was driven to extinction. For this reason, some states now have laws against keeping bullfrogs in captivity.

Housing

In the wild, bullfrogs prefer large stagnant bodies of water with a profusion of water plants at the shallow margins. They are large and active animals, capable of leaping up to nine times their body length.

In captivity, they require large roomy cages with equal areas of land and water. The land area must be at

Bullfrogs are the largest frog in North America.

least two square feet with a substrate of damp moss or leaves. The water must be deep enough for the frog to float at the top without touching the bottom. Because bullfrogs are native to temperate regions, no heaters or aeration are necessary.

In cool weather, bullfrogs will bury themselves in leaf litter to hibernate, but they can be kept active throughout the winter if maintained at normal temperatures.

Feeding

Bullfrogs have enormous appetites and will often lunge at food that is obviously too big to swallow. Like all frogs, their vision is acutely attuned to small moving objects, which they will instantly snap up in their cavernous jaws.

In the wild, bullfrogs will eat nearly anything, including insects,

mice and even small birds. They will also eat each other, and individuals of different sizes should not be kept together. A captive adult bullfrog will require a minimum of 60 or 70 crickets per week as food.

Breeding

Bullfrog breeding requires a large enclosure and is most often accomplished in outdoor frog ponds. They only breed in areas containing areas of thick aquatic vegetation. Male bullfrogs may be recognized by their eardrums; in males, the eardrum is noticeably larger than the eye, while in females the eye and the eardrum are roughly the same size.

During the summer breeding season, male bullfrogs become very territorial and will attack intruder frogs; the frogs will face each other

and try to push each other onto their backs.

After amplexus, up to 20,000 eggs may be laid which, strangely, are among the smallest eggs laid by any frog. Depending on water temperature, the eggs hatch in one to three weeks into green tadpoles with black speckles. The tadpoles will usually take at least two years to complete their metamorphosis. The newly emerged froglet is about one and a half inch long and reaches sexual maturity about two years after metamorphosis at an age of four years. They can reach a length of six inches at an age of seven years.

Cuban Tree Frog (Hyla septentrionalis)

Level: Novice
Size: Small
Habitat: Tropical, Arboreal

Biology

Cuban tree frogs are native to the Caribbean Islands but have been introduced elsewhere by hitchhiking in fruit crates and imported plants. A breeding population has now been established in Florida.

Cuban tree frogs are the largest tree frogs in North America, reaching a length of over five inches. Like most tree frogs, they can change color according to temperature and mood. They are usually

Large and active frogs, Cuban tree frogs need a good-sized cage.

nocturnal, spending the day resting against tree trunks and walls. Cuban tree frogs have enormous toe pads and are excellent and active climbers.

Housing

Cuban tree frogs will do well in a typical tree frog setup, including a tangle of tree branches and plants for climbing, a soft damp substrate with a shallow water dish and warm humid conditions. They are large and active, and accordingly they require somewhat bigger cages than other species. They also need somewhat warmer conditions to match their tropical habitats with daytime temperatures in the 80s and nighttime lows in the mid-70s. Cuban tree frogs are cannibals and will eat any smaller frogs, including other Cuban tree frogs. They should only be housed with other frogs of approximately the same size.

Feeding

Cuban tree frogs are active predators and voracious feeders. In the wild, they will eat anything they can catch and swallow, including insects, small lizards and other frogs. They are capable of catching and swallowing even such large prey as green tree frogs. Captives should not be housed with smaller frogs. A good diet consists of crickets which have been dusted with vitamin and mineral supplements,

but like all frogs, Cuban tree frogs do best if they are offered a wide variety of food items.

Breeding

In the wild, Cuban tree frogs breed throughout the summer in any standing body of water, including temporary pools and drainage ditches. Captive breeding is very difficult and has rarely been successful. The females, at an adult size of five and a half inches, are almost twice as big as the adult males. Froglets are marked with bright white dorsolateral stripes, which soon disappear.

Giant Toad
(Bufo marinus)

Level: Intermediate
Size: Medium
Habitat: Tropical, Terrestrial

Biology

As the name suggests, the giant toad is one of the largest living anurans. It is native to Central and Latin America but has been widely introduced into other parts of the world, including Florida, Hawaii and Australia. Introduced giant toads, referred to as cane toads or marine toads, are a serious threat to indigenous species, and as a result some areas have laws against keeping this species.

In appearance, the giant toad is distinguished by the large paratoid glands located behind the eyes, which, as in all toads, secrete a milky poisonous liquid. If the paratoid gland is squeezed, the giant toad can eject a stream of toxin up to a foot away. The poison is not particularly powerful, but the toad secretes so much of it that it can be lethal to predators that try to swallow it. Captives grow quite tame and do not usually exude toxin unless handled very roughly. However, the giant toad should always be handled with care, and contact with the toxin should be avoided.

The giant toad's toxic secretions can be lethal to its predators.

Housing

Since adult giant toads may measure up to eight inches from nose to vent and weigh up to four pounds, they require large roomy accommodations with a deep substrate of leaf litter and several hiding places. The substrate should be kept damp, but there should also be a place for the toad to dry off completely. Like all toads, they do not drink from a dish but obtain water by absorbing moisture through the thin skin on their bellies. A shallow water pan provides a suitable soaking spot and will help keep the humidity at the required level.

Because the giant toad is a tropical animal, it requires daytime temperatures in the low 80s, dropping to the mid-70s at night. They are not very effective leapers and do not require a lid as long as their tank is higher than ten or twelve inches.

Feeding

Giant toads are essentially eating machines with appetites that match their large size. In the wild, they will eat virtually anything that moves and that can fit into their mouths. Captives will eat crickets, beetles, worms, small mice and other frogs and toads. The giant toad is also a cannibal and will eat other toads and frogs as well as smaller individuals of its own species. An adult giant toad requires at least seventy crickets or two or three small mice per week.

The saliva of the giant toad is a mild paralytic and acts to numb and paralyze rodents and other small prey so they can be safely swallowed by the toad.

Breeding

Although giant toads breed easily in the wild and can soon reach plague proportions, they have proven to be difficult to breed in captivity. In the wild, they can breed any time that conditions are suitable, usually during the tropical rainy season from July to October. If conditions remain good, Giant toads can breed every month. The eggs hatch in about three days, and the tadpoles complete their metamorphosis after about forty-five days. During her fifteen-year life span, a single female toad can produce an enormous number of offspring.

Green Toad (Bufo viridis)

Level: Intermediate
Size: Small
Habitat: Desert/Savannah, Terrestrial

Biology

Green toads are native to the arid regions of Europe and northern Africa. They can tolerate lower temperatures than most other frogs and are frequently found at higher elevations.

An adult green toad reaches about four inches in length and can be distinguished from other toads by the greenish cast of its skin, which varies in intensity according to temperature and mood.

The green toad is hardy and easy to care for but is unfortunately somewhat rare in the pet trade.

Housing

Green toads have housing requirements similar to those for American toads. Although the green toad is native to arid regions, it does require some moisture in the form of a spot of damp substrate or moss. It will also soak itself in a shallow water dish if one is available and can tolerate even somewhat brackish water. No external heat is required, although a heat source may become necessary if winter temperatures are too low.

Feeding

Green toads are eclectic feeders and will take all sorts of small invertebrates and insects. A diet of crickets makes a good staple, although these should be fortified with a vitamin and mineral powder and should also be supplemented with a variety of other live prey. Earthworms are also eagerly accepted.

Breeding

Green toads are similar in their breeding habits to most other toads. Mating takes place in a confused mass of toads gathered in shallow water, and the males will usually grasp at anything that looks remotely toad-like. The eggs are laid in long jelly-like tubes, which hatch in a few days and produce small black tadpoles. Metamorphosis takes place a few months later, and the toadlets usually emerge from the water during a rainy night.

Green Tree Frog
(Hyla cinereus)

Green tree frogs grow so quickly that they may need to shed their skin every other day.

Level: Novice
Size: Small
Habitat: Tropical, Arboreal

Biology
Green tree frogs are native to the subtropical areas of the southeastern United States. They are usually a light apple-green color, but like most tree frogs, they change color according to the temperature, becoming darker when cold. They are one of the largest tree frogs in North America, reaching a length of two and a half inches and grow rapidly, often shedding their skin every two days.

The green tree frog is usually found on the stems of water plants in stagnant water, often no more than two or three feet above the water surface. This frog is probably the most commonly kept of the tree frogs.

Housing
Like all tree frogs, green tree frogs are highly arboreal and seldom descend to the ground. They require large cages with at least as much vertical space as horizontal and with a profusion of plants and tree branches to climb on. Daytime temperatures in the low 80s are suitable, dropping to the 70s at night.

Although green tree frogs from the northern part of their range will bury themselves in the substrate and hibernate if it gets too cool, they can be kept active throughout the winter if their tank is kept at normal temperatures. A shallow water dish will help maintain the desired humidity, but this should not be too large, as the frogs swim very poorly and could drown. The cage should be misted every morning. Because they are active climbers and escape artists, a tight-fitting lid is a necessity.

Feeding
Green tree frogs are active nocturnal hunters, who spend most of the day asleep in a protected spot, emerging at night to hunt for insects. In the wild, they feed largely on spiders and mosquitoes, pouncing on them from distances up to three or four feet. Captives can be fed houseflies, small crickets, beetles and ants. Like all frogs, they do best when fed a wide variety of insect food.

Breeding
Male green tree frogs can be recognized by their distinctive breeding call, which sounds somewhat like a duck. In the wild, the breeding

season begins in March and lasts all summer. The frogs are much more likely to call just before a storm, a habit which has earned them the nickname of "rain frogs."

The brown and yellow eggs are laid in clumps that are attached to the stems of plants in shallow water. The tadpoles complete their metamorphosis in about two months.

Grey Tree Frog (Hyla versicolor and Hyla chrysoscelis)

Level: Novice
Size: Small
Habitat: Temperate, Arboreal

Biology

There are actually two species of grey tree frog, *Hyla versicolor* and *Hyla chrysoscelis,* which are virtually impossible to tell apart. The *chrysoscelis* species seems to have

appeared as a result of a mutation, which gives it twice the normal number of chromosomes, a phenomenon known as "polyploidy." Although they have different numbers of chromosomes, the two species look virtually identical and can often be found living in the same habitat (or even the same tree).

Grey tree frogs are arboreal and rarely descend to the ground. They are capable of significantly changing their skin color, becoming darker grey or greenish as the temperature drops. Their coloring also serves as a natural camouflage, making them appear as a lump of lichen on a tree branch, and this is their main defense against predators. If threatened, they will leap into space with their fingers and toes widely outstretched. Their digits have sticky pads at the tips, and they are capable of stopping their fall if even a single toe touches a passing branch.

Grey tree frogs are excellent climbers, and a tight-fitting cage lid is a necessity.

Grey tree frogs are nocturnal and are most active in early evening. They are native to the eastern half of the United States.

Housing

Grey tree frogs are arboreal and active, requiring large cages with vertical space and lots of branches for climbing. A tight-fitting lid is necessary—they are excellent climbers. Like all frogs, they require a high humidity, and their cage must be misted every day to allow them to absorb moisture through their thin skin. They are not effective swimmers and rarely enter the water, but a shallow water pan in their cage will help to keep the humidity at acceptable levels. A substrate of moss or damp soil is best with subdued lighting. They are native to the temperate climate of the United States, and thus they prefer unheated terrariums with a daytime temperature in the high 70s or low 80s, dropping at night to the low 70s. Normal room temperatures are acceptable for them. Grey tree frogs have extraordinary tolerance to cold climates, and during severe winters, they can produce a glucose solution within their bodies which serves as a natural antifreeze.

Feeding

Grey tree frogs, like all frogs, are insectivorous and feed on whatever arthropods or flying insects they can catch. In the wild, their diet consists largely of mosquitoes, flies and other semi-aquatic insects. They are fast and acrobatic hunters and will often leap into mid-air to catch flying insects on the wing, seemingly with little forethought as to where they will land. They will also sometimes descend to the ground to catch and eat small worms or crawling insects. Captives do best on a diet of houseflies, small crickets, pillbugs or other insects. Mealworms should be avoided as their hard shells are difficult to digest. Fly maggots should be avoided as well because they are sometimes capable of surviving in the stomach and causing damage. A good way to feed the frogs is to place a small light bulb in the cage and set it outside in the evening with a large screen mesh lid. Insects will enter the cage, attracted by the light, and will be quickly snapped up by the frogs.

Breeding

Grey tree frogs breed in the late spring with the males starting their characteristic calls (a high-pitched flutelike trill—faster in the *chrysoscelis* species) in the early afternoon along the edges of ponds and slow-moving streams. During this time, they can be easily captured using a flashlight. Males may be recognized by their darker throat and slightly larger tympanum (the best way to recognize a male, of course, is the fact that only males will sing).

The leopard frog closely resembles the toxic pickerel frog—frequently fooling predators that steer clear.

The egg mass (which may contain up to 1,000 eggs) is a brown or tan mass of jelly which is laid in shallow water. The tiny tadpoles hatch in about two days and complete their metamorphosis after about sixty days. They are attractive animals with a metallic color and a bright orange or red tail. At the time of metamorphosis, the froglets measure about one half inch long and reach an inch or so in length before their first winter. The young frogs reach a breeding size at an age of three years.

Leopard Frog
(Rana pipiens)

Level: Novice
Size: Small
Habitat: Temperate, Semi-Aquatic

Biology

The leopard frog is very similar in appearance to the pickerel frog but can be distinguished by its round spots rimmed with a white outline, in contrast to the squarish markings of the pickerel frog. Because the leopard frog looks so much like the toxic pickerel frog, it is often confused with it by predators who have learned to avoid pickerel frogs, and thus the leopard frog gains some measure of protection, a phenomenon known as "Batesian mimicry."

Leopard frogs inhabit the areas near cool woodland streams, but also wander into fields and grasslands, thus earning the name "meadow frog." The leopard frog tolerates a very wide range of habitats and is found virtually throughout the United States, where it has developed several geographical races or subspecies.

Housing

The housing accommodations for the leopard frog are typical of that for most frogs. A ten-gallon aquarium will provide enough space to hold an adult frog comfortably.

The tank should be divided into a land area and a water area. The land area should be provided with a moss substrate and a piece of bark or rocks to serve as a hiding place.

The aquatic portion of the tank should be large enough for the frog to swim and deep enough for the frog to float with its eyes protruding but without having its feet touch bottom. The water does not have to be heated or aerated, but it should be changed regularly. The frogs will spend most of their time in the land area but will leap into the water whenever they are frightened. They will also occasionally soak themselves, floating with just the tops of their heads above the surface.

Lighting should be subdued, and the frogs should be kept at room temperature or slightly lower. A tight-fitting lid is necessary to prevent escapes.

Feeding

The leopard frog can be fed in much the same manner as any other typical frog. In the wild, most of its food consists of woodland insects, worms and other invertebrates. Captives can be fed a diet of crickets, but as these are deficient in several necessary nutrients, they should be dusted with commercially available supplement powder. Leopard frogs also do best if they are offered a wide variety of prey, ranging from grasshoppers and crickets to houseflies, beetles

and worms. A diet of four or five crickets (or their equivalent) per day is sufficient to keep them in good health.

Unlike most frogs, leopard frogs are genetically programmed to slow down their body metabolism in wintertime and hibernate, even if they are kept artificially warm. Most captive leopard frogs will therefore not eat at all during the winter but will retreat to the bottom of the aquatic portion of the tank, or bury themselves under the moss substrate, to hibernate. They will feed again in spring.

Breeding

Throughout most of their range, leopard frogs breed in the spring, when the males gather in shallow pools or ponds and give their mating calls, which sound like the familiar low guttural croaking of most frogs. Like all frogs, male leopard frogs are capable of croaking even underwater.

After amplexus, the frogs lay masses of up to 500 black and white eggs among the leaves of water plants, enveloped in a thick jelly-like mass. In captive breeding, the eggs should be carefully removed and incubated in a shallow tank of water. They will hatch two to four weeks later, depending on the temperature. The green and black tadpoles develop legs after about thirty days and will complete their metamorphosis six to eight

weeks later. The froglets reach sexual maturity in about two years.

Leopard frogs breed readily in captivity and as a result are widely available as pets. They are also used in large numbers as laboratory animals and for dissections in biology classes.

Oriental Fire Bellied Toad (Bombina orientalis)

Level: Novice
Size: Small
Habitat: Temperate, Semi-Aquatic

Biology

Oriental fire bellied toads are native to China and Japan. They are members of the discoglossid family of frogs and lack an extendable tongue. The brilliant red and black colors on the belly serve as a warning, as this frog has a powerful toxin in its skin. When threatened, the frog will assume a characteristic position with its back arched and its chin held up to display the strikingly colored stomach. The toxin can cause intense pain and burning if it is accidentally rubbed into the eyes. Oriental fire bellied toads should be handled rarely or not at all, and the hands should always be thoroughly washed after handling them.

Captive-bred Oriental fire bellies are rarely as bright in color as wild-caught specimens because their diet in captivity is often deficient in the pigment canthaxanthin, which produces the brilliant red color.

The European fire bellied toad, a close relative with yellow and black on the belly, is sometimes available in the pet trade. It is cared for in the same manner as the Oriental fire bellied toad.

Housing

Oriental fire bellied toads are more aquatic than the true toads and require tanks with approximately equal areas of land and water. The water should be six or eight inches deep and need not be aerated, but it must be replaced often. Otherwise their toxic skin secretions may build up to such a concentration as to kill them. Oriental fire bellied toads are best kept in a single-species tank since they may inadvertently poison their tankmates with their powerful skin toxins.

Because they are native to the mountainous areas of Japan and China where they thrive in stagnant ponds and pools, Oriental fire bellied toads do not require high temperatures and do well at ordinary room temperatures or even slightly cooler temperatures. The land area should be covered with moss or leaf litter, and this must be misted often to keep it from drying out. Hiding places in the form of pieces of bark or rock caves must

be provided, and overcrowding should be avoided.

Feeding

Oriental fire bellied toads will eat insects and aquatic invertebrates of all sorts, including crickets, beetles and small worms. They can even tackle small fish, swallowing them a bit at a time as they are digested. They have no extendable tongue, and therefore they must capture their prey by leaping upon it with open jaws, using the forelimbs to stuff the food into their mouths. They are active and fast and will consume large amounts of food if it is available.

The diets of captive Oriental fire bellied toads tend to lack the pigment canthaxanthin, which is found in their natural foods, and thus captive frogs tend to lose their colors over time. This can be prevented by feeding captive frogs freshwater crustaceans such as fairy shrimp and red worms, which contain large amounts of pigment. There are also

commercial pigmented-food supplements available for tropical fish and birds such as flamingoes, and these can be added to the frog's food to help maintain its bright colors.

Breeding

Oriental fire bellied toads breed fairly easily in captivity as long as conditions are to their liking and a natural seasonal cycle of light and temperature is maintained. The male frogs can be recognized by their thicker forearms and the rougher skin on their backs.

Breeding takes place more or less continuously throughout the summer. The toads breed in the water with the males calling constantly during the warmer months. When a receptive female approaches, the male grasps her around the waist in amplexus. Females lay approximately 100 eggs per clutch, which rest on the bottom of the tank. Adult frogs will sometimes eat the eggs of other individuals,

Due to their toxic secretions, Oriental fire bellied toads should be handled rarely or not at all.

and the newly laid eggs should be carefully removed from the tank and placed in a separate hatchery, consisting of a layer of gravel and water. The eggs hatch in eight to ten days, and the tadpoles complete their metamorphosis around three weeks later. Young Oriental fire bellied toads reach sexual maturity in about two years.

Pac Man Frog
(Ceratophrys ornata)

Level: Intermediate
Size: Medium
Habitat: Tropical, Terrestrial

Biology
Pac Man frogs are native to Latin America where they inhabit the damp leaf litter on the rain forest floor. In appearance and habits, they are very similar to the African bullfrogs, but they are not closely related. This appearance of a common body structure and habits in response to similar environmental conditions is known as "parallel evolution."

These frogs are referred to in the pet trade as "Pac Man frogs" (after the popular video game character) because of their huge heads and mouths, which sometimes look as though they are nearly half of the frog. Their somewhat menacing appearance is heightened by their large size. A full grown Pac

The Pac Man frog gets its name from its large head and mouth.

Man frog can reach the size of a grapefruit in just a few years. They are unusual among frogs in having a full set of teeth on both jaws, which they use to ambush their prey. Although not normally aggressive, they have very strong jaw muscles and large specimens can give a painful bite if disturbed.

Housing
Despite their large size, up to seven inches from nose to vent, Pac Man frogs are not active animals and do not require large accommodations. A large adult can be kept comfortably in a ten-gallon aquarium. They prefer a daytime temperature in the low 80s, dropping to the 70s at night. Subdued lighting is best with a typical equatorial light schedule of twelve hours of light and twelve hours of dark. A deep substrate of leaf litter or moss must be provided, into which the Pac Man frog will bury itself, leaving only the horned eyes protruding. Because they do not swim well, the water dish should be shallow enough for the frog to climb out using its short stumpy legs, and the water should be just deep enough to cover the frog's belly. The substrate should be kept thoroughly damp and must be misted every morning to keep the necessary high humidity. Pac Man frogs must be kept in a single species tank, as they will eat nearly anything that moves, including smaller frogs.

Feeding
In the wild, Pac Man frogs feed largely on other frogs, which they ambush with their large powerful jaws. Large captive Pac Man frogs

can be fed small frogs such as green tree frogs, which are readily available in pet stores. They will also eat newborn mice or rats, known as "pinkies," as well as large salamanders or small lizards. Younger Pac Man frogs can be fed earthworms or smaller salamanders. Insects such as crickets will be accepted but should not be used as a staple diet as they do not contain the large amounts of protein needed by these frogs.

Prey items must be live—the frogs will be attracted by the movement and seize the prey in their strong jaws, crushing it and using their front limbs to push it into the throat.

Their large jaws and extendible stomachs make Pac Man frogs capable of taking prey that is almost as large as they are. Pac Man frogs have appetites to match their large size and should be fed often (one pinkie mouse every two or three days).

Breeding

The breeding behaviors of Pac Man frogs are not well understood, and they are not often bred in captivity. On those occasions where they have bred, mating and egg-laying has been induced by the injection of hormones. The tadpoles, unlike those of most frogs, are carnivorous and have large powerful jaws. They feed on small aquatic vertebrates, including each other.

Pickerel Frog
(Rana palustris)

Level: Novice
Size: Small
Habitat: Temperate, Semi-Aquatic

Biology

The pickerel frog is a common inhabitant of cool woodland streams in the eastern United States. As the name indicates, it was once widely sold as fishing bait and has been introduced to many areas outside its native range.

It is very similar in appearance to the leopard frog and shares the same habitat, but the pickerel frog can be distinguished by its generally browner coloration, the orange coloration on the underside of the rear legs and its large squarish spots, in contrast to the round white-rimmed spots of the leopard frog. The pickerel frog is wary and will leap to safety at the slightest disturbance, but its primary defense lies in the toxins secreted by its skin. The toxin is not lethal to predators but is strong enough to make them sick, and thus they learn not to attack pickerel frogs.

The pickerel frog has an adult size of about three inches from snout to vent. It is diurnal and hunts during the day and is agile enough to sometimes climb onto low shrubs or branches.

Housing

Pickerel frogs are not as aquatic as some of the other ranid species, although they are not often found far from water and will retreat into it when alarmed, diving under the surface and hiding themselves in the muddy bottom or under rocks. The land area of their tank must therefore be a bit larger than the aquatic area. If provided with hiding places in the form of rocks or pieces of bark, pickerel frogs are somewhat sedentary in captivity and will spend most of their time waiting for prey to wander by. Their thin skin is easily damaged, and the substrate must be covered with a layer of moss or leaf litter. The water area should be deep enough for the frog to float without its feet touching bottom.

Because of their powerful skin toxins (which are fatal to other frogs), pickerel frogs must be kept in a single-species tank. Their water must also be changed often, as the toxins can accumulate to levels high enough to kill the frogs with their own poison.

Feeding

Pickerel frogs, like all frogs, are insectivores and will eat nearly anything that moves that is small enough to swallow. In the wild, they will eat water-loving arthropods such as gnats, mosquitoes, flies, butterflies, beetles, caddis flies and small dragonflies. Captives do well with a staple food of crickets. This diet should be supplemented with a variety of live foods to provide a nutritional balance—houseflies, millipedes, beetles and the like. The diet should be carefully controlled, because pickerel frogs have unending appetites and will eat constantly if allowed, to the point where they may grow obese and unhealthy. A typical adult pickerel frog needs about four or five crickets per day.

As with all frogs, the feeding response in pickerel frogs is triggered by the sight of a small erratically moving object, and dead insects will not be recognized as food.

Breeding

Pickerel frogs breed after the spring thaw from mid-April to early May in most parts of their range. They gather in ponds and pools by the thousands to breed and lay eggs. The males can be recognized by their loose throat sacs and their mating call, which sounds somewhat like a rusty door hinge. Mating takes place in the water with the male grasping the female around the waist until the yellow and brown eggs are laid.

The eggs form a round jelly-like mass about three inches in diameter. Each mass is attached to an underwater plant or rock and contains up to 500 eggs. The tadpoles are green with tiny black spots. They metamorph into inch-long froglets after about four months.

Poison Arrow Frog (Dendrobates species)

Level: Intermediate
Size: Small
Habitat: Tropical, Semi-Arboreal

Biology

Few animals are as spectacularly colored as the poison arrow frogs from the Latin American rain forests. Their bright colors serve as a warning, for these little frogs produce some of the most powerful toxins found in nature. As the name suggests, natives in the Amazon River Valley use the skin toxins to poison their blowgun darts. Although the toxin is not dangerous unless it enters the bloodstream, it is extremely powerful and can cause death quickly. For this reason, poison arrow frogs are not for the beginning herper, and captive poison arrow frogs should be handled only if absolutely necessary and then only with a net—never with bare skin.

Aside from these precautions in handling, poison arrow frogs can be kept in much the same manner as any other arboreal tropical frog. They are extraordinarily bold and will often prowl around their cages in open daylight, hunting small insects. Poison arrow frogs can live up to ten years in captivity.

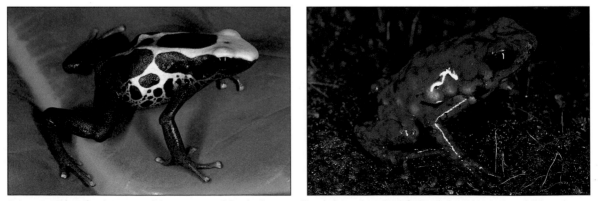

Poison arrow frogs produce some of the most powerful toxins in nature (*Dendrobates tinctorius*, left; *Dendrobates histrionicus*, right).

Housing

Poison arrow frogs are native to the rain forests of Latin America and require warm and humid conditions. They are largely arboreal and so require tall cages with a profusion of branches and wide-leaved plants for climbing. They also require a number of hiding spots on the ground. Male frogs are territorial and will fight each other over desirable locations, so the cage should be large enough for each individual to establish his own territory.

They need a high humidity but cannot tolerate stagnant air, so the cage must be well-ventilated. Shallow pans of water placed in the tank will keep the humidity acceptably high, but because poison arrow frogs cannot swim at all, these dishes must be shallow and well-supplied with pebbles or logs to enable the frogs to climb out without drowning.

The powerful skin toxins can easily poison other tankmates, so poison arrow frogs should never be kept with other species. The substrate and water must be changed often to prevent a lethal buildup of skin toxins.

Feeding

Poison arrow frogs, while very small, are active, have large appetites and will eat a surprisingly large amount of food. In the wild, they subsist mostly on tropical ants, but captives will accept small insects such as baby crickets or flies. Like all frogs, they will only eat live prey. Food insects should be dusted regularly with vitamin and mineral powders.

Captive poison arrow frogs tend to lose their potent skin toxins after a few generations of breeding, and this is believed to be caused by the lack of some necessary environmental factor. One theory is that the frogs use the formic acid found in the bodies of many tropical ants to help manufacture their alkaloid skin toxins, and lose the ability to produce toxins if not fed their native diet.

Breeding

Poison arrow frogs are not difficult to breed in captivity, provided that their environmental conditions are suitable. The males are territorial and each will claim a particular branch or rock for singing. The call is quacklike. The male will attempt to mate with any female that enters his territory. In the wild, the eggs are laid inside the dish-shaped Bromeliad plants, but captives will lay in small shallow dishes of water. Adults will eat each others' eggs— so if more than one breeding pair is kept, the eggs should be removed and hand-raised. The eggs hatch in about two weeks. The tadpoles, unlike those of most frogs, are carnivorous and can be fed fish food, brine shrimp or small amounts of egg yolk. They grow quickly and metamorph in about two months. The froglets reach breeding size in about two years.

South African Bullfrog (Pyxicephalus adspersus)

Level: Intermediate
Size: Medium
Habitat: Tropical, Semi-Aquatic

Biology

The South African bullfrog, which is not closely related to the familiar American bullfrog, is one of the largest frogs in the world and may reach a length of eight inches from snout to vent. They are also known as "Pixie frogs," a reference to the scientific name. In appearance and habits, they are very similar to the Latin American horned frogs or "Pac Man frogs," an example of what is known as "convergent evolution," in which animals on different continents develop similar body structures and habits in response to similar environmental conditions.

South African bullfrogs are creatures of the wet rain forests of southern Africa where they bury themselves in the deep leaf litter with just their eyes protruding, waiting for prey to pass within range. They have short legs and cannot leap very well, and thus they use their strong jaws to defend

South African bullfrogs are best kept in their own aquarium, as they will eat anything that moves, even members of their own species.

themselves if threatened and are capable of giving a painful bite if disturbed. They are, fortunately, very placid animals and rarely attempt to bite once they have adjusted to their captive conditions.

Housing
South African bullfrogs are quite sedentary animals and do not move around much. A ten-gallon aquarium is sufficient for even a full-grown specimen. They are best kept in solitary confinement, as they will eat anything that moves, even each other.

Although they require damp conditions and a high humidity, they have short, stumpy legs and swim very poorly or not at all, and if their water dish is too deep, they can easily drown. A wide shallow water pan with water no more than one half inch deep is best. South African bullfrogs require deep moist substrates, either moss or decomposing leaf litter, in which they will scoop out a depression and bury themselves up to their eyeballs. This should be misted regularly to keep the humidity at acceptably high levels.

African bullfrogs prefer subdued light or shade with daytime temperatures in the low 80s. A tropical light schedule of twelve hours on and twelve hours off is best.

Feeding
South African bullfrogs are ambush hunters and will wait for prey to wander within range.

Like all frogs, they are very sensitive to motion and leap upon their prey as it approaches, seizing it in their strong jaws and crushing it before using the forelimbs and the eyeballs to push it down the throat. A full-grown South African bullfrog will eat virtually anything that it can fit into its mouth. In the wild, they have been known to eat even such large prey as full-grown rodents and birds. They have appetites to match their size and will often lunge at prey that is obviously far too large to swallow.

Captives require a large amount of high-quality food to provide their need for protein. A good staple food consists of very young mice, known as "fuzzies." These are big enough to satisfy the frog's appetite without being a danger to the frog. African bullfrogs will also eat large insects such as locusts or amphibians such as salamanders or other frogs.

Breeding
South African bullfrogs are not often bred in captivity. It is known that in the wild the female frog will guard her clutch of eggs, lunging even at human observers in order to defend them. The tadpoles are also watched over by the females.

Ironically, once the froglets emerge after metamorphosis, they are eagerly snapped up and eaten by the larger adults.

Tadpoles, All Species

Level: Novice
Size: Small
Habitat: Varies according to species, Aquatic.

Biology

During the spring and early summer, tadpoles of all types can be found in nearly any permanent body of water, usually in the warmer shallow areas near shore. Many tadpoles look alike—often the only method of positive identification is to raise them until they undergo metamorphosis. In general, frog tadpoles are greenish or brownish, while toad tadpoles tend to be black. In addition, most frog tadpoles have their vent opening at the right side of their tails, while toad tadpoles have the cloacal vent on the centerline.

All tadpoles lack eyelids and have a horny parrotlike beak rather than jaws. Gills are present rather than lungs, and these are covered with skin, with water entering through a hole known as a spiracle. During the metamorphosis process, the gills are absorbed as the lungs take over, and the front limbs develop and emerge through the spiracle. Tadpoles may take from several weeks to several years to undergo metamorphosis, depending on the species.

Housing

Tadpoles are totally aquatic and require nothing more than several inches of water and a pile of rocks for hiding. No heaters are needed for most species, but the water should be aerated with an ordinary aquarium pump and airstone. Most species need about a gallon of water per individual. The larger tadpoles, such as the bullfrogs or leopard frogs often found in pet stores, require at least five gallons each.

As the limbs begin to appear, the tadpole will want to leave the water briefly, and a floating log or pile of rocks must be provided to allow the tadpole to crawl out. Once metamorphosis is complete, the froglet or toadlet should be moved to more terrestrial accommodations.

Feeding

Nearly all tadpoles are herbivorous with the exception of a few carnivorous species like horned frogs and spadefoot toads. They will graze on algae growing on the rocks, logs and glass sides of the tank, which they will scrape off with their rasped tongue and strong-beaked mouths. This diet can be supplemented occasionally with boiled lettuce or spinach.

As metamorphosis approaches, the tadpoles will prefer some meat in their diet and can be fed on small worms or commercial fish pellets. Newly emerged froglets are insectivorous and can be fed on small insects such as baby crickets, houseflies or fruit flies until large enough to take adult foods.

Breeding

Although larval salamanders are sometimes capable of developing

Nearly all tadpoles will eat algae growing on the rocks, logs and sides of their tank.

sex organs and breeding, no known species of frog is neotenic, and no known species of tadpoles are capable of breeding.

White's Tree Frog
(Litoria caerulea)

Level: Novice
Size: Medium
Habitat: Savannah, Arboreal

Biology

White's tree frog, one of the largest tree frogs in the world, is native to the south Pacific Ocean. These frogs are common in Australia, but due to the country's strict regulations protecting its native reptiles and amphibians, most of the White's tree frogs available in the U.S. are imported from New Guinea. A few are captive-bred from imported individuals. They are often sold under the name "dumpy frogs," a reference to their folded skin and their rather forlorn-looking expressions. They are large and heavy frogs with a distinctive bright green skin that shines with a thick waxy coat (which helps prevent water loss). In the wild, they are found in semi-arid areas where other tree frogs would have a difficult time surviving.

Although large, White's tree frogs are quite docile and sedentary, and tolerate handling much better than most frogs. The toe pads are very large, and help the frog climb about in its hunt for food.

White's tree frogs have noticeably large toe pads. Although generally a bright green color, this specimen is displaying the frogs' "blue phase."

Housing

White's tree frogs, though quite large, are not very active animals and do not require large accommodations. They are exclusively arboreal and rarely descend to the ground; thus, the cage should have plenty of vertical space and a large number of plants and tree branches should be provided for climbing. The frogs will prefer to spend most of their time in a shady damp corner, venturing out once in a while to hunt for food.

Because they are quite capable of capturing and swallowing smaller tree frogs, they should be housed either alone or with frogs that are roughly the same size. They prefer warm temperatures in the high 70s or low 80s with subdued lighting.

The thick waxy coating on their skin helps them to retain body moisture, and they can therefore tolerate drier conditions than most other tree frogs. However, they will also do well in more humid conditions. Their cage should be misted every morning. A tight-fitting lid is necessary to prevent escapes.

Feeding

White's tree frogs can get big enough to overpower and swallow such large prey as small rodents and other frogs, but they do well in captivity on a diet of grasshoppers, crickets, moths and other large insects. These are pursued by leaping through leaves and branches until they are caught in the large jaws. Large amounts of insect food will be eaten.

White's tree frogs have good dispositions, soon become very tame and can often be hand-fed by holding a live cricket or other insect in front of them. A good way to feed them is to place them in a cage with a wide screen top, add a piece of meat or ripe fruit, and set the cage outside in the shade. Flies and other insects will be attracted to the bait, enter the cage through the screen, and be snapped up by the waiting frogs.

White's tree frogs will also capture and eat smaller frogs, and should be kept only with frogs of their own size.

Breeding

White's tree frogs have been bred in captivity but not reliably. Little is known about conditions for captive breeding. On those occasions in which breeding has been successful, the frogs laid up to 300 eggs in water, and these have hatched within a day or two. The tadpoles develop quickly and emerge as froglets after about a month.

If well fed, the froglets grow quickly and can reach a size of two inches within two or three months. If conditions are suitable, White's tree frogs may mate several times during the summer.

Wood Frog
(Rana sylvatica)

Level: Novice
Size: Small
Habitat: Temperate, Terrestrial

Biology

The wood frog is native to the woodlands of eastern North America. It is sometimes referred to as the "robber frog" because of its dark eye markings. Wood frogs can vary their colors according to their mood and temperature—in warm weather they are tan or light brown, turning blackish green in cooler surroundings.

Wood frogs range farther north than any other frog and are even found within the Arctic Circle in Canada. Their extraordinary tolerance to cold is the result of a natural defense mechanism against freezing. In cold weather, the frog produces a glucose solution within its body that acts as a natural antifreeze. While the frog's intercellular

fluids may sometimes actually freeze solid, the glucose cryo-protectant prevents the cells from freezing, enabling the frog to survive until warmer weather. Wood frogs can also tolerate drier conditions than most frogs, often ranging long distances from water.

The wood frog is said to be more intelligent than other frogs.

Housing

Wood frogs do well in a typical woodland terrarium with a damp moss substrate and several pieces of bark or rocks to provide hiding places. The cage should be misted daily. They prefer a natural lighting cycle with subdued light or shade, and thrive at ordinary room temperatures. In winter, they may bury themselves in the substrate to hibernate, but they can be kept active if the temperature is kept artificially high at room temperature.

Although wood frogs in the wild are often found far from water, they enjoy soaking in a shallow

Ranging farther north than any other frog, wood frogs can be found in Canada's Arctic Circle.

water dish where they can absorb moisture through the thin skin on their bellies. They will also often climb onto low branches and shrubbery in pursuit of insect prey, and their cage can be provided with a number of horizontal tree branches.

Wood frogs are medium-sized animals, reaching an adult length of about three inches from snout to vent. A ten-gallon aquarium will hold two or three frogs comfortably.

Feeding

Wood frogs are typical insectivores. In the wild, they will eat all sorts of woodland arthropods, from beetles and pill bugs to small worms and salamanders. Captives can be raised on a diet of houseflies and small crickets, supplemented by beetles, millipedes and other arthropods. Three or four crickets per day are sufficient intake for them. Like all frogs, their vision is attuned to small moving objects, and they will only accept live insect prey.

Although wood frogs can live peaceably with other frogs of the same size, they should not be kept in the same cage as very small froglets. Because they are not very large, wood frogs should not be housed with larger frogs of other species, as they may be attacked and eaten.

Breeding

Wood frogs are early breeders in the wild, often mating as early as March or April. The males gather in ponds and shallow pools and call to the females for a period of two or three weeks. The call is a short explosive clacking sound that may be repeated several times in a row. The males can be recognized by the larger webbing on their rear feet.

After amplexus, the female lays a globular mass containing some 3,000 chocolate brown and white eggs, which quickly turn green due to a growth of algae within the jelly-like envelope that surrounds them. The eggs can take anywhere from three or four days to over a month to hatch, depending on the temperature. The newly hatched tadpoles are greenish-black in color. The froglets emerge from the water after two or three months. If the eggs are laid late in the season, the tadpoles may overwinter before completing their metamorphosis in the following spring. The newly emerged froglets are about three quarters of an inch long.

CHAPTER 3

Salamanders

L ike all amphibians, salamanders begin their lives as aquatic larvae with gills before turning into terrestrial adults. The newts and salamanders together make up the amphibian order Caudata, or "tailed ones."

The word "newt" is generally used to denote those Caudata that spend their adult lives in water, while "salamander" refers to those which, while aquatic as young larvae, leave the water upon adulthood and take up a terrestrial existence. But to a biologist, there is no distinction between the aquatic and terrestrial forms; both are members of the order Caudata and can be referred to collectively as "salamanders."

The spotted salamander is a member of the "mole salamander" family.

Plethodontids

This is the largest of the salamander families with about 225 species found in North and South America. All members of this family lack lungs and breathe through their thin moist skin. The majority of the members of this species are found in the northeastern United States. The plethodonts include such familiar species as the red backed salamander, slimy salamander and the ensatina. The whole family is largely terrestrial, and many lay eggs on land, which hatch as fully formed young salamanders. One species, the arboreal salamander from California, lives almost exclusively in trees.

Ambystomatids

Heavy-bodied secretive burrowers, the "mole salamanders" family includes many familiar animals such as the spotted salamander and the tiger salamander. There are about thirty species, all of them found in North America and Mexico.

Salamandrids

Six species are found in the United States, including the Oregon newt, California newt and the red spotted newt. Most of the forty-five species in this family are found in Europe.

Amphiumids

The Amphiumas are aquatic amphibians that somewhat resemble eels with small front limbs. The family contains three species, which differ in the number of toes.

All are found exclusively in North America.

Cryptobranchids

In addition to the American hellbender, this family also includes the giant salamander of China and Japan, which, at a length of almost five feet, is the largest living amphibian. The hellbender is the largest amphibian in North America.

Necturids

Five species including the mudpuppy and its relatives make up this family, all of them found in North America. They are aquatic animals with gills that never leave the water. The mudpuppies are neotenic, which means they carry the characteristics of juvenile salamanders and keep them throughout their adult life.

Sirenids

There are two genera of sirens, found only in North America. They are totally aquatic and resemble eels with tiny front limbs. In size, they range from the dwarf siren, which barely reaches one foot in length, to the greater siren, which can reach three feet or more.

Dicamptodontids

This family includes the Pacific giant salamander and its relatives. Found exclusively in the American Pacific Northwest, there are three species that range from three to

The greater siren can grow to over three feet in length.

eight inches in length. Largely restricted to cool streams and seepages, however, the giant salamander will occasionally ascend into trees.

Natural History

The Caudata are one of the oldest living groups of terrestrial vertebrates. The salamanders developed from the labrynthodonts, the very first vertebrates to venture onto land in the Devonian period some 350 million years ago. The labrynthodonts were descendents of a group of fishes known as rhipidistians, or "lobe-finned" fishes. Among the unique characteristics of the rhipidistian fishes was a skull bone pattern that closely matches that of the earliest-known amphibians. In the rhipidistian fish *Osteolepis,* for example, there are two bones at the roof of the skull that correspond to the parietal bones in terrestrial vertebrates, and between them is an opening for the pineal gland or "third eye," which in terrestrial animals serves as a light indicator to calibrate the internal clock.

By far the most important feature of the rhipidistians, however, was their lobed fins, which consisted of two pairs of fleshy projections with a rayed fin at the ends.

The giant salamander of China and Japan is the largest amphibian on Earth.

Each lobe contained a number of bones and muscles that enabled the fin to be moved, allowing the fish to propel itself along the river bottom (somewhat similar to the modern "walking catfish").

The rhipidistian lobe fin was most highly developed in the later species, including *Eusthenopteron*. *Eusthenopteron* differed from most other rhipidistians in having a number of bony projections from its vertebral bones, which gave increased protection to the spinal cord.

In the upper Devonian period, some 375 million years ago, the earliest known terrestrial vertebrate appeared, called *Icthyostega*. *Icthyostega* had well-developed limbs with five toes, just as all other land vertebrates. The *Icthyostega* limbs had a skeletal structure consisting of a single large upper bone (called the humerus in the front limbs and the femur in the rear) and two long bones in the lower limb (called the radius and ulna in the front limbs, and the tibia and fibula in the rear limbs). The digits and "wrists" are made up of a large number of smaller bones. This pattern is also found in every other terrestrial animal. The fleshy lobe fins of the rhipidistian fishes have an identical bone structure, which corresponds one to one with the limb skeletons of *Icthyostega* and other terrestrial vertebrates.

In addition to its five-fingered limbs and other obvious amphibian characteristics, however, *Icthyostega* still possessed a number of characteristics unique to its rhipidistian fish ancestors. The most apparent of these was a large rayed fin, like a fish's, along the rear edges of the tail. The bony fin supports found in *Icthyostega* are identical to those found in the rhipidistian tail fins. *Icthyostega* also retained small scales in its skin, a trait characteristic of the rhipidistian fishes but not of amphibians, which have smooth, unscaled skin.

The vertebral bones of *Icthyostega* were also nearly identical with those of the rhipidistian fishes. Although each vertebral bone possessed a bony projection or "process," the vertebra were loose and not tightly connected to each other as they are in all other terrestrial animals. Because terrestrial animals need a strong solid backbone in order to support the weight of the body against gravity, this suggests that, despite the five-fingered limbs, *Icthyostega* had still not become efficient at terrestrial locomotion and probably spent most of its time in the water (as would be expected from a fish-amphibian transition), using its limbs to push itself around on the river bottom. This belief is confirmed by the presence in the *Icthyostega* skeleton of canals for the lateral line organ used by fish to sense vibrations in the water.

The first fossil salamander to be uncovered by naturalists was found in Germany in 1725 but was misidentified at the time as the skeleton of a human who had perished in Noah's Flood. Today, it is dated to the Miocene period, about 15 million years ago, and is given the scientific name *Andrias scheuchzeri*. It is an ancestor of the modern giant salamander of Japan and China.

The earliest recognizable salamander in the fossil record is a seven-inch skeleton found in Kazakhstan in the former USSR, which dates to around 140 million years ago. The fossil, named *Karaurus*, is believed to have evolved from a group of labrynthodonts known as branchiosaurs. Most of the modern salamander families appear to have evolved in the area that is now the eastern United States. About 300 species of salamander are alive today, just a tiny fraction of the great amphibian diversity that once existed.

Biology and Anatomy

Salamanders are often mistaken for lizards, but they can be distinguished by their smooth moist skin, the lack of claws on their toes and the lack of a visible ear hole.

Larval salamanders look much like their parents except that they have gills. Unlike frog tadpoles, salamander larvae have four well-developed legs which they use for swimming.

Salamanders are ectotherms (their bodies take on the temperatures of their surroundings), but they have a greater tolerance of colder temperatures than do reptiles. Salamanders do not seem to be capable of regulating their body temperature through behavioral methods; they do not move from areas that are too cold for them, for example, but remain until they die. For this reason, it is estimated that some 50% of all salamanders die during hibernation. Contrary to myth, salamanders cannot survive in fire.

Salamanders are not active animals, and during its lifetime, an individual salamander may not move more than a mile.

Gills

Although nearly all salamander larvae possess gills, these are usually lost at adulthood. In a few families, however, the adults are also entirely aquatic, and they retain the gills. The gills are somewhat similar to those of fish and are richly supplied with blood vessels. The thin walls of these vessels allow oxygen to diffuse into the blood from the surrounding water. Since cold water can hold more dissolved oxygen than warm water, salamanders that live in cooler water do not need large gills, while those living in warmer waters must develop large bushy bright red gills in order to extract enough oxygen.

Skull

Salamander skulls lack any ear openings, and no outer or middle ear is present. As a result, all newts and salamanders are completely deaf to airborne sounds. Instead, the remnants of the ear bones are connected to the animal's shoulder girdle, which allows it to sense faint vibrations carried to it through the legs. Salamanders are almost totally dependent, however, on their keen senses of smell and taste to provide them with information about their surroundings.

Tongue

The salamander tongue serves two purposes. It is richly packed with nerve endings, and its sense of taste is very sharp, allowing the salamander to follow scent trails to track down prey or to find a potential mate. The sense of taste is particularly well-developed in the aquatic newts.

The tongue also functions as a means of capturing prey. In many terrestrial salamanders, the tongue can be extended like that of a frog, sometimes to a distance of half the body length. The sticky mucus on the end helps trap small insects or worms.

Eyes

Salamanders, being largely nocturnal, have little need for visual acuity and thus have extremely poor eyesight. The tiny eyes can sense nearby movement but cannot discriminate shapes or forms—and probably cannot distinguish colors

Salamanders have no ear openings and are completely deaf (palm salander).

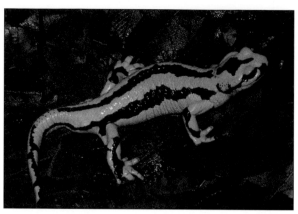

As a rule, brightly colored skin indicates that a salamander exudes a strong toxin (fire salamander).

either. Aquatic species that inhabit murky waters have particularly bad eyesight. In species that habitually live in total darkness, such as the cave salamanders, the eyes have virtually disappeared and have become covered with skin to the point of being nonfunctional. Salamanders rely on their extraordinary sense of smell to find prey.

Lungs

While most salamanders and newts possess functional lungs as adults, a large number do not. The aquatic species, such as the Amphiuma or mudpuppy, retain their gills throughout their life span and never leave the water. The skin of salamanders and newts is thin and permeable, and these animals are able to supplement their oxygen intake by diffusing air through their skin. This method is the only one used during hibernation. The members of the plethodon family of terrestrial salamanders, which contains some 60% of all living salamanders, have lost their lungs completely and breathe solely through their moist skin.

Skin

Like all herps, salamanders must periodically shed their skin to grow. The old skin peels off in patches and is usually eaten. In many aquatic species, the skin is shed in minute pieces, sometimes one cell at a time. Unlike frog skin, the skin of salamanders is attached tightly to the body.

Salamander skin contains numerous glands that serve several purposes. A large number of mucus glands keep the skin lubricated and moist. The mental gland, located on the chin, secretes chemicals called pheromones which serve as a sexual signal. Finally, all salamanders secrete toxins in their skin to protect against predators, and those species with the strongest toxins usually have bright warning colorations. These toxins also function as fungicides and parasite removers.

Pelvic Girdle

Like lizards, salamanders' legs are located at the sides of the body and project straight outward. They walk by moving one leg at a time in a diagonal pattern. In many salamanders, though, the legs are not strong enough to support the body weight, and the belly is dragged along on the ground. In these species, locomotion takes the form of a serpentine wriggling motion, particularly if the salamander is attempting to move quickly. To jump, most salamanders use the both the rear feet and the tail to push themselves into the air.

Cloaca

The cloaca in salamanders serves as the common exit point for the digestive, urinary and reproductive tracts. In most salamanders, the male is distinguished by a swelling of the cloacal lips. Salamanders are unique among amphibians in practicing a form of internal fertilization. During mating, the male deposits a packet of sperm called a spermatophore, which the female then picks up using the lips of her cloaca. This spermatophore is then stored and used to fertilize the eggs before they are laid. Thus, fertilization in salamanders is internal even though there is no direct cloacal contact.

Tail

Salamanders, like lizards, are capable of voluntarily shedding their tails as a defense mechanism if they are threatened. The detached tail jumps and twitches violently due to muscle contractions and diverts the attention of a predator long enough to allow the salamander to escape. The lost tail soon grows back. Salamanders have remarkable regenerative powers that are unique among vertebrates. They are capable of regenerating lost toes and even whole limbs, and because the locomotion of the salamander isn't dependent upon its legs, the loss of a limb doesn't handicap the salamander until it grows back.

Diseases

Chemical Poisoning

Salamanders are extremely sensitive to chemicals in their environment, and their tanks should contain distilled or rain water rather than tap water. Disinfectants containing pine oil or soap should never be used to clean a newt's or salamander's cage, as they are quickly lethal to the animal.

Wounds

Salamanders should be handled rarely if at all and then only with wet hands to avoid damaging the skin. Skin tears easily become infested with fungus, which appears as tufts of white cottony material. This can be treated by soaking the salamander in a weak iodine or Bactine solution several times a day. Betadine, an antiseptic that is commonly used on reptiles, is toxic to amphibians and should not be used.

In crowded conditions, salamanders may attack each other and bite off tails, toes or even entire limbs. This is not as disastrous as it looks, as salamanders have extraordinary regenerative powers and can regenerate a lost toe or even a lost limb.

Leprosy

Crowded conditions can result in a condition called "salamander leprosy," where the skin splits and bleeds, and the toes and tail rot and drop off. It particularly attacks the toes and feet. The condition can sometimes be treated using broad-spectrum antibiotics produced for fish.

Mouth Rot

This is similar to the disease found in snakes and other reptiles but is caused by a different bacterial organism. The lower jaw swells and becomes discolored. Death follows quickly if not treated. The medicinal drugs commercially available for treating "fin rot" in tropical fish are effective. Place a few drops of medicine in a small tank of water and soak the salamander twice daily for ten or fifteen minutes.

Species Descriptions

Japanese Fire Bellied Newt (Cynops pyrrhogaster)

Level: Novice
Size: Small
Habitat: Temperate, Semi-Aquatic

Biology

Japanese fire bellied newts are native to cool mountain streams in Japan and China. They can tolerate cold much better than most salamanders and are often found at high elevations.

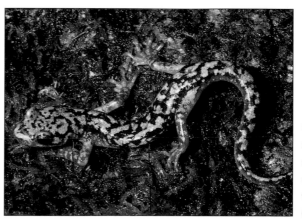

Like frogs and toads, salamanders have sensitive skin and must be handled with great care (green salamander).

The bright red and black bellies are a warning coloration, as these newts possess a powerful toxin in their skin. In addition to protecting them from predators, the skin toxin also serves as an anti-bacterial and helps prevent fungus infections and parasites from attacking the skin.

Japanese fire bellied newts have lived up to twenty-five years in captivity.

Housing

Japanese fire bellied newts are almost entirely aquatic and seldom leave the water. Although they prefer cool temperatures, they can tolerate a wide range of water conditions, provided that there are no sudden changes. They do best in a semi-aquatic terrarium with a small land area, consisting of rocks covered with a layer of moss or dead leaves and a large water area at least eight inches deep. Underwater rock caves should be provided as hiding places. A gravel substrate can be used, but it is not required. The water need not be heated or aerated, because Japanese fire bellied newts prefer cooler conditions. Some aquatic vegetation should be provided, especially if breeding is being attempted.

Feeding

Japanese fire bellied newts eat worms, frog eggs and small insects in the wild. They can also capture and eat small fish. Captives can be fed a diet of tubifex worms, blood worms, sinking fish food pellets, shrimp pellets and small pieces of raw meat. Japanese fire bellied newts often become tame enough to accept food from the fingers.

Breeding

Breeding Japanese fire bellied newts is not difficult as long as conditions are suitable. A well-planted, well-aerated tank is required, and breeding individuals must be allowed to undergo a period of hibernation prior to breeding.

During the breeding season, male newts develop rough dark skin patches on their rear thighs and a high tail crest as a sexual signal. The courtship ritual is elaborate and takes place in the water. The male uses his tail to wave scent from his skin glands toward the female. After a time, the male will

HELP HERPS

Animal smuggling is a very big business. An easy way for criminals to avoid the law is to smuggle animals into a country that has not signed the CITES agreement and to then export the animal legally. Don't be a victim of this activity and don't encourage it. Make sure that any herp you obtain was either captive-bred or was not brought into the country illegally.

deposit a spermatophore on the substrate, which the female will pick up with her cloaca. The eggs are laid one at a time among water plants. They hatch in a few days.

Mandarin Newt (Tylotriton shanjing)

Level: Novice
Size: Small
Habitat: Temperate, Semi-Aquatic

Biology

This large, striking salamander is native to China and eastern Asia. It is also known as the emperor newt. Although not often seen in the United States, this salamander is popular in Europe and was at one point exported so heavily that the species was exterminated in some parts of its range.

The Mandarin newt reaches lengths of up to eight inches as an adult. The ground color is black or dark brown, but the body is marked with dazzling orange stripes and large bright spots along the rib cage. As with most brightly colored herps, the Mandarin newt's gaudy color scheme is a warning signal, for its skin contains a collection of poisonous alkaloids that are distasteful to predators. Despite this protection, some members of the water snake group are immune to the toxin and regularly feed on these newts.

The Mandarin newt's skin contains a number of poisonous alkaloids.

The eggs hatch in about three weeks and produce small free-swimming larvae. After about five months, the larvae complete their metamorphosis and emerge as young adults about two inches long.

Marbled Salamander (Ambystoma opacum)

Level: Intermediate
Size: Small
Habitat: Temperate, Terrestrial/Burrower

Housing
Mandarin newts are largely terrestrial but require damp conditions with areas of freestanding water. A typical terrestrial setup such as that used for slimy salamanders or red backed salamanders can be used, as long as a shallow water bowl is also provided. A number of rocks and branches should be provided to allow easy access, because these newts do not swim particularly well.

Mandarin newts are native to cool mountain areas in the Far East, and they can be kept at typical room temperatures and do not require any external heat sources. They are largely nocturnal and prefer subdued lighting.

Feeding
Like all salamanders, Mandarin newts are predators that forage on the forest floor for small invertebrate prey. Captives can be fed earthworms, waxworms and small insects. These should be dusted with commercial vitamin powders to provide a complete diet. Unlike most newts, Mandarin newts will not usually eat food while underwater.

Breeding
The Mandarin newt is not widely bred in the United States, but it is the subject of much captive breeding in Europe.

As with all newts, breeding takes place in the water. The males can be recognized by the swollen cloaca lips, which are much larger than those of the female. The mating ritual involves much wrestling and prodding on the part of the male. About two weeks after mating, the female will lay up to seventy-five small eggs on an underwater rock.

Biology
Although marbled salamanders are one of the smaller salamander species, (reaching lengths of up to four inches), they are nonetheless heavily built. They are found in damp woodlands in the eastern half of the United States. They prefer habitats that are close to ponds or streams but seldom enter the water, preferring somewhat drier surroundings. Marbled salamanders spend most of their time in burrows or hiding under rocks or logs. They are very placid animals, seldom moving fast even if uncovered. They are not particularly uncommon but are seldom seen because of their secretive habits.

Housing
Marbled salamanders can be housed in a typical woodland terrarium containing several inches of

moist humus or potting soil. This should be covered with a layer of damp moss or dead leafs, and hiding places should be provided in the form of flat rocks or pieces of bark. The cage must be misted every day to keep the substrate damp. Marbled salamanders will do well at ordinary room temperatures and do not require any supplemental heat. They should not be housed with any smaller salamanders.

Feeding

Marbled salamanders are typical woodland salamanders and feed on small worms, insects, millipedes, slugs and snails. Captives can be fed blood worms or small earthworms as well as baby crickets.

Breeding

The breeding habits of the marbled salamander are unique in several ways. Unlike most salamanders, which breed in large congregations during the spring thaw, marbled salamanders mate and lay their eggs in the fall and do not form large breeding colonies. They are also unusual in that they lay their eggs on land rather than water. The female selects a spot in a depression or ditch and lays a clutch of fifty to 100 eggs, then curls around them to protect them and keep them moist. When the autumn rains come, the eggs are flooded and hatch a few days later. The grayish-colored hatchlings are just three quarters of an inch long, but grow quickly and undergo metamorphosis before the cold weather sets in. Newly emerged adults measure about two and one-half inches. If there is not enough rain to hatch the eggs, they will overwinter and hatch the following spring.

Marbled salamanders spend most of their time in hiding.

Red Backed Salamander (Plethodon cinereus)

Level: Novice
Size: Small
Habitat: Temperate, Terrestrial

Biology

The red backed salamander is the most common salamander in the eastern United States. One experimenter in New Hampshire found over 1,200 salamanders—most of them red backs—in just one acre of woodland. This works out to one and one-half pounds of salamanders per acre, a greater biomass than even birds at the peak of their breeding season.

Red backed salamanders are found in two color phases, the normal red back, with a red stripe on the dorsal side, and the lead back, which is plain grayish-black without a stripe. Both color forms can occur in the same clutch of eggs.

Red backed salamanders have extraordinary tolerance for cold climates and are found as far north as the Arctic Circle in Canada. During the winter, they hibernate under logs or in underground chambers. To help prevent them from freezing, red backed salamanders are capable of losing most of their body moisture during hibernation.

Housing

Probably every child has at one point captured a handful of red backed salamanders and tried to keep them in a bucket of water, only to find them dead in the morning. Red backs cannot swim well and never enter water voluntarily.

They can be kept in a woodland terrarium, with one or two inches of dirt covered with a layer of damp moss or leaf litter. Hiding places must be provided in the form of rocks or pieces of bark. A water dish is not necessary, since the salamanders can tolerate somewhat dry conditions and would only drown themselves in standing water. The substrate must be misted with water every morning to keep it damp.

Red backed salamanders can tolerate cool conditions and do not require any supplemental heat. They will thrive at room temperatures, and will remain active throughout the winter. A ten-gallon aquarium provides sufficient space for a colony of ten red backed salamanders.

Feeding

Red backed salamanders will eat virtually any sort of small arthropod or invertebrate, including slugs, small earthworms and insects, including foul-tasting prey that other salamanders won't touch. Captives can be fed blood worms and small earthworms, and can sometimes be trained to eat small pieces of raw beef or liver.

Breeding

Like many plethodonts, red backed salamanders are entirely terrestrial and do not enter water, even to breed. Mating takes place in the early spring, but the fertilized eggs are not laid until late in the fall. Six to twelve eggs are laid in a bundle that looks somewhat like a bunch of grapes, attached to the roof of a tiny cavity in the soil or in a rotted log. The female stays with the eggs until they hatch to protect them from predators and to keep them moist. Most females only breed every other year.

Red backed salamanders have no aquatic larval stage—when the eggs hatch in two months, they produce perfectly formed miniature salamanders less than one inch long. The young stay with their mother for a short time before wandering off on their own. They reach sexual maturity in about two years, at a length of about two and one-half inches.

Red Eft
(Notopthalmus viridescens)

Level: Novice
Size: Small
Habitat: Temperate, Terrestrial

Biology

Red efts are the terrestrial juvenile stage of the red spotted newt. Their color ranges from a bright orange to a dull brick red, but the bright red spots are a conspicuous warning signal, for red efts secrete a strong toxin in their skin which protects against predators and also helps control fungus and parasite infections. They can be found in damp woodlands all over the eastern half of the United States and often boldly walk around in broad daylight, especially after rainstorms—protected by their noxious skin secretions. They can tolerate dry conditions and are often found as far as one-half mile away from water.

After a period of one to three years, the efts begin to turn from a reddish to an olive green color and migrate to a stream or pond to transform into an adult.

Housing

Red efts are very hardy animals and do not require elaborate housing. They can be kept in a typical woodland terrarium such as that used for red backed salamanders. They require a damp substrate of moss or leaf litter, which must be sprayed with water periodically. They do not drink water but instead absorb it through their thin skins.

Unlike most salamanders, red efts are diurnal and active during the day, where their spectacular colors stand out vividly against a moss background. They are active and inquisitive, become very tame and tolerate gentle handling.

Feeding

Red efts are active feeders and spend most of the day rooting through leaf litter in search of small forest invertebrates. In the wild, they will eat slugs, small worms, springtails and pill bugs. Captive specimens will eat blood worms or small earthworms, and will sometimes accept small pieces of raw liver or beef. They will eat a surprisingly large amount of food for their small size.

Breeding

Although some salamanders can breed as juveniles, the red eft is not known to be capable of developing sexual organs until it reaches adulthood and enters the water. In some areas, aquatic larval red spotted newts may reach sexual maturity as aquatic adults without passing through the eft stage, but no red spotted newts are known to be neotenic.

Red Spotted Newt (Notopthalmus viridescens)

Level: Novice
Size: Small
Habitat: Temperate, Semi-Aquatic

Biology

Red spotted newts are widespread throughout the eastern half of the United States. Because they are common and easy to care for, they are often used as laboratory animals and have been sent aloft in the space shuttle to test the effects of weightlessness. They are also very common in the pet trade, where they are sold as "green newts" or "common newts." Pets that have been liberated or escaped have established breeding populations in many non-native areas.

The adults are almost totally aquatic and rarely leave the water. They possess lateral-line sensing organs like fish for detecting vibrations in the water and can rise or sink by altering their buoyancy utilizing a bubble of air in their bodies. Red spotted newts do not possess gills, however, and must surface occasionally to breathe air. The juvenile stage, the red eft, is terrestrial and rarely enters the water.

Housing

Unlike the juvenile red efts, adult red spotted newts are almost completely aquatic and rarely leave the water. They prefer cool water with subdued lighting, a dense growth of plants and a pile of rocks for hiding places. The water should be at least six or seven inches deep to provide plenty of swimming area, but the tank need not be aerated or heated.

Red spotted newts are protected from most predators by their potent skin toxins, but their eggs are vulnerable to predation, thus the newts are not usually found in bodies of water that contain fish. They can be safely kept, however, with other species of newts, including Japanese fire bellied newts, California newts and Oregon newts. They can tolerate quite low water temperatures and can often be found swimming under the ice in winter, prowling for food.

Feeding

Like all salamanders, red spotted newts are carnivorous predators. In the wild, they hunt down small aquatic animals such as leeches, snails, worms and small crustaceans. They also eat large amounts of frog eggs. Captives will accept tubifex worms, sinking fish food pellets or small pieces of raw beef or liver. They have large appetites and will eat a surprising amount of food.

Breeding

Red spotted newts are spring breeders, gathering in thickly planted areas in April and May. During the breeding season, the males develop a high tail fin as a sexual signal and rough dark patches of skin on the insides of the legs, which help him grip the female during amplexus. After a ritualized mating display, the female lays about 400 eggs among the stems of water plants. These hatch in three to eight weeks into tiny half-inch long larvae.

The gilled larvae grow quickly, developing legs soon after they hatch and emerging as terrestrial red efts in about three months. The efts remain in their terrestrial stage for several years before adopting the adult color scheme and returning to the water.

Slimy Salamander
(Plethodon gluttinosus)

Level: Intermediate
Size: Small
Habitat: Temperate,
Terrestrial/Burrower

Biology
The slimy salamander is one of the most widespread of the eastern plethodon lungless salamanders, as well as one of the largest. Adult slimies may reach seven inches or more in length, although they are rather slender-bodied. The color scheme of glossy black skin speckled with white spots acts as camouflage, making the salamander appear as a fungus-infested twig or stick. The camouflage spot patterns are unique to each salamander and can be used to tell individuals apart.

The slimy salamander's primary defense against predators, however, is its thick skin secretion, which clings like glue to anything it touches and makes the salamander unappetizing to predators. Slimy salamanders are elusive, secretive and usually seen only during rainstorms when they prowl around the forest floor. Like all plethodonts, they lack lungs and breathe completely through their moist skin.

Every slimy salamander has its own individual pattern of spots.

Housing
Slimy salamanders are woodland creatures, inhabiting the leaf litter in forests throughout the eastern United States. They prefer wetter conditions than most of their plethodont cousins and are seldom found far from water. In captivity, they do well in a typical woodland terrarium with a layer of damp soil covered with moss or leaf litter and plenty of hiding places in the form of rocks or pieces of bark. A shallow water dish will help keep the humidity high enough, but the water dish should be filled with pebbles or pieces of wood to enable the salamanders to crawl out (if they fall in), because they cannot swim. The substrate must be misted every morning to keep it damp.

Slimy salamanders are territorial, and each individual will establish a territory surrounding a particular rock or hiding place, from which they will not venture more than a few inches. They are best housed in a large tank with plenty of room, and then only with salamanders of their own size.

Feeding
Slimy salamanders are large and active predators that hunt through leaf litter for small invertebrates. In the wild, they eat insects, worms, slugs, and other salamanders, including smaller individuals of their own species. Captives will eat worms and slugs and can sometimes be trained to accept small pieces of raw beef or liver.

Breeding
Although the courtship and breeding habits of the slimy salamander

have been the subject of much scientific study, breeding these salamanders in captivity is difficult and is rarely attempted. At sexual maturity, male slimies are around six inches long, while the larger females can reach up to seven inches.

During courtship, the male rhythmically raises and lowers his body while nudging the female with the scent gland on his chin. The male will then move along the female's body until his tail is under her chin, and then vibrates the tail, stimulating the female to climb atop his tail. The male then deposits a spermatophore which is picked up by the female.

Like all plethodonts, slimy salamanders lay eggs on land in groups of twelve to thirty-six in a rotted log or under a rock. The female stays with the eggs until they hatch. Slimy salamanders have no larval stage—the young hatch from the egg as miniature versions of their parents. They reach sexual maturity in about three years.

Spring Salamander
(Gyrinophilus porphyriticus)

Level: Intermediate
Size: Medium
Habitat: Temperate, Semi-Aquatic

Biology
Spring salamanders, growing to a length of eight and one-half inches, are one of the largest of the lungless salamanders. They are much more aquatic than other salamanders and are rarely found far from water. With their streamlined bodies and their flattened tails, they are powerful swimmers.

The spring salamander used to be known as the purple salamander. At one time not much was known about their life in the wild, and they were known largely through pickled specimens, which often turned purple when placed in preservative. The most conspicuous marking is a light line extending from the nostrils to the upper lip, which marks the location of a groove which carries scent particles from the ground to the nose.

Like most salamanders, spring salamanders are very dependent upon their chemical senses. The tongue of the spring salamander is somewhat unusual, being attached at the middle and free at both ends. The tongue is used as a sensory organ as well as an aid in swallowing prey.

Housing
The spring salamander is almost exclusively aquatic and prefers shaded areas with cool running water. Although they swim well, they spend most of their time hiding under rocks or pieces of bark at the water's edge, ready to dive into the water and swim away if disturbed. They are largely nocturnal, emerging at night to hunt for food.

They will occasionally wander overland during heavy rainstorms.

Captives must be provided with shallow, cool water, a large number of rocks and hiding places and a small land area with a moss or leaf substrate. Spring salamanders are efficient hunters and should not be housed with smaller salamanders, even smaller members of its own species.

Feeding
Spring salamanders are large and have powerful jaws. In the wild, they eat small fish, earthworms and smaller salamanders. Captives can be fed earthworms, slugs and small snails. They can sometimes be taught to accept pieces of raw liver or beef. Spring salamanders will attack any smaller salamanders that share their tank.

Breeding
Spring salamanders require exacting conditions to breed and are not often bred in captivity. In the wild, they breed in the spring, laying between ten and 100 eggs attached to submerged rocks. These hatch in late summer into gilled larvae about three quarters of an inch long. These grow slowly, and a spring salamander may spend up to three years as a larva before undergoing metamorphosis. Newly metamorphed adults are about four inches long. They are ready to breed in another year or two.

Tiger Salamander
(Ambystoma tigrinum)

Level: Novice
Size: Medium
Habitat: Temperate, Semi-Aquatic

Biology

The tiger salamander is one of the most common amphibians in North America with at least seven subspecies distributed throughout the United States. The western subspecies tend strongly toward neoteny, in which the larva do not undergo metamorphosis but are capable of breeding without turning into adults like the axolotl. Larval tiger salamanders are often sold in pet shops under the name "mudpuppy" or "waterdog," but they are not closely related to the true mudpuppies. Both the larvae and the adults of the tiger salamander are widely sold as fishing bait and have been widely introduced to non-native areas.

They do well in captivity and become quite tame, reaching lengths up to thirteen inches and living for as long as twenty-five years. Their large size, undemanding dispositions and bright yellow and black colors have made them popular pets. Although they are large and docile, tiger salamanders have delicate skin which is easily injured and should not be handled.

Housing

Juvenile or larval tiger salamanders are entirely aquatic and require nothing more than six or seven inches of water and some rocks to hide in. They can tolerate ordinary room temperatures and do not require heated water, although they may need the extra oxygen provided by an airstone and pump. After several years, the larva will lose its gills, develop the adult color pattern and emerge from the water.

Once it undergoes metamorphosis, the adult tiger salamander can be kept in a typical woodland terrarium with a thick substrate of leaf litter or moss and plenty of hiding places. If provided with a shallow water dish, they may enter it occasionally.

Tiger salamanders are normally quite secretive and seldom venture far from their burrows, but in captivity, they soon overcome their shyness and become responsive pets.

Feeding

Tiger salamanders have large appetites to match their large size and emerge from their hiding places at night to hunt down insects, worms, slugs and smaller salamanders. The aquatic juveniles can be fed worms, sinking fish food pellets or small fish, as well as pieces of raw beef or liver. Terrestrial adults will eat insects, worms and smaller salamanders, and can usually be taught to accept pieces of raw meat, which they will sometimes take from their keeper's fingers. Because they are large and powerful hunters, they should not be housed with amphibians that are smaller than they are.

With their beautiful coloring and pleasant dispositions, tiger salamanders have become popular pets.

Breeding

Tiger salamanders have been bred in captivity but usually only in large outdoor ponds that provide seminatural conditions. The males are usually larger than the females. Breeding takes place in the spring after the first rains. The eggs are laid in packets attached to the stems of water plants in nearly any permanent body of water.

The hatchling larvae are about one-half inch long and reach a length of four inches by late summer when the metamorphosis process begins. The western sub-species have a strong tendency towards neoteny, in which the larvae do not undergo metamorphosis but reach sexual maturity as larvae. Those individuals who do undergo metamorphosis emerge from the water at a length of four or five inches and take up a terrestrial existence. They reach sexual maturity in about a year.

Two Lined Salamander (Eurycea bislineata)

Level: Novice
Size: Small
Habitat: Temperate, Semi-Aquatic

Biology

Two lined salamanders are the most common of the brook salamanders, which are found only in the eastern half of the United States. Like all

Two lined salamanders are particularly fun to keep because they are active during the day.

brook salamanders, two lines prefer to live near cool shallow streams and springs. The northern populations of two lined salamanders tend to be larger in size than those individuals from the south.

Unlike most salamanders, two lined salamanders are largely diurnal and active during the day. They spend most of their time searching along the shore for food. Two lined salamanders are excellent swimmers and will escape into the water if threatened, using rapid wriggling movements of the body to propel themselves into the water. They are very vulnerable to predators, however, and are not usually found in waters where fish live.

Housing

In the wild, two lined salamanders prefer much wetter conditions than most salamanders. Although not strictly aquatic, two lined salamanders are rarely found far from water. They prefer cool shaded woodland streams. In captivity, they require several inches of cool water that is kept in motion by bubbling air through an aquarium pump using an airstone. A pile of rocks with a moss substrate will provide the necessary shoreline, and hiding places must be provided in the form of pieces of bark or leaf litter. The salamanders will spend most of their time resting under objects along the water's edge. Two lined salamanders are not aggressive and can be safely housed with newts and other small salamanders.

Feeding

Two lined salamanders feed almost exclusively on small worms, which they find under rocks at the water's edge. Captives can be fed tubifex worms or blood worms as well as small earthworms.

Breeding

Two lined salamanders breed in spring after a complicated courtship ritual which takes place entirely underwater. The male rubs the female with a scent from the mental gland on his chin before the female straddles his tail and presses her chin against the base of his tail. The male then deposits his spermatophore, which is then picked up by the female in her cloaca. Up to 100 eggs are laid on submerged rocks, and the female sometimes stays near them to drive away potential predators. The hatchling larva are about one-half inch long and remain in the larval state for two to three years before undergoing metamorphosis at a length of almost two inches. Full-grown adults measure five or six inches from nose to tail.

PART III

Reptiles

Turtles · Lizards · Snakes

Turtles

All turtles are members of the very primitive anapsid group of reptiles, meaning that they have solid skulls with no spaces or holes between the bones. Together, the 200 species of turtles make up the order of reptiles called Chelonia, which is further divided into two groups; the cryptodirans (characterized by their ability to pull their heads into their shells by folding their neck vertically) and the pleurodirans (or "side-necked turtles," who retract their heads under the margin of their shells by folding their necks sideways).

The vernacular term "turtle" refers to any member of the chelonians. The word "tortoise" is usually used to refer to those chelonians that are primarily terrestrial, while the name "terrapin" is usually applied to those turtles that are largely aquatic in habits. These names have no scientific standing, however; to a biologist, all shelled reptiles are members of the Chelonia order, and all chelonians can be referred to as "turtles."

Cryptodirans

Chelydrids

This family contains the common snapping turtle and its subspecies, as well as the alligator snapper. The Chinese big headed turtle is also sometimes placed in this group, while other taxonomists classify it as a separate family, the platysternids. While once a thriving and widespread family, the chelydrids are now all but extinct.

Emydids

Including about eighty species, this is the largest of the existing turtle families. They are found nearly everywhere except Australia and Madagascar. Most of the aquatic sliders, cooters, map turtles and pond turtles are in this family. It also contains the Asian and North American box turtles. The greatest diversity in the family is found in the northeastern United States.

Dermatemydids

This is a single-species family containing the tabasco turtle, a large river turtle from Central America. This old and once-diverse family is now virtually extinct.

Testudinids

This family contains the forty-one species of terrestrial tortoises, which are found in dry warm areas on all continents except Australia. The largest living land turtle, the Galapagos tortoise, is a member of this family. It also includes the hingeback tortoises and the various

The Galapagos tortoise is the largest living land turtle. The Galapagos can reach over four feet in shell length and can weigh over 500 pounds.

mediterranean tortoises commonly found in the pet trade. The gopher and desert tortoises are the only North American members.

The alligator snapper is one of the remaining members of the chelydrid family of turtles.

The toad-headed turtle is a member of the side-necked family.

Kinosternids

This group contains the twenty-three species of mud and musk turtles. They are found only in North and South America. Although the kinosternids look like small snappers, they are not very closely related.

Stauroptypids

These three species of Mexican musk turtles were formerly classed with the kinosternids but have now been placed in a separate family of their own.

Carretochelyds

The carretochelyds were once a widespread and successful family, but today only one species still survives, the Fly River turtle of Australia. This is a large aquatic turtle similar in habits to the softshells.

Trionychids

The trionychids are a large family consisting of the softshell turtles. The family contains about twenty-five species, three of which are found in the United States. Others are found in Mexico, Asia and Africa. All are aquatic.

Scientists are in the process of dividing the large *Trionyx* genus of softshells into a number of smaller genera, including *Apolone.*

Cheloniids

The sea turtles family includes the Ridley's turtle, green turtle, hawksbill and loggerhead. There are six species, which are widely distributed in tropical seas. All of them are listed as threatened or endangered species.

Dermochelyids

This family contains a single species—the marine leatherback turtle. Unlike most turtles, the leatherback lacks a carapace and instead has a covering of thick leathery skin. Its main food consists of jellyfish. The leatherback is the largest living turtle.

Pleurodirans

Pelomedusids

The African snake-necked turtles have extremely long and flexible necks, which they use to snare fish.

Chelids

The side-necked turtles are found in Latin America. The best-known

The matamata is the best-known of the side-necked turtles.

member of this family is the mata-mata, a large aquatic turtle found in the Amazon River Basin.

Natural History

Turtles are one of the oldest reptile groups still in existence. The exact ancestry of turtles is still in dispute, but it appears likely that they evolved from the primitive cotylosaurs, or "stem reptiles," which appeared during the Pennsylvanian period some 300 million years ago. Two possible ancestral groups (based on skull similarities) are known as romeriids and pareiasaurs.

The earliest recognizable turtle, known as *Triassochelys,* comes from the Triassic period, just as the dinosaurs began to flourish almost 200 million years ago.

Several other fossil turtles have been found from the age of the dinosaurs, including the land turtle *Proganochelys* and the giant marine turtle *Archelon,* which, at twelve feet, is the largest turtle that ever lived. The largest terrestrial turtle lived in Africa and Asia and is known as *Colossochelys.* It resembled the modern Galapagos tortoise but was almost twice as big and weighed more than a quarter ton.

When the dinosaurs died out at the end of the Cretaceous period, 65 million years ago, most turtle families died out with them. The few turtles that survived the extinction are the ancestors of modern chelonians. The 230 living species of turtles can thus be considered as "living fossils."

Biology and Anatomy

The most readily apparent characteristic of turtles is, of course, their shells. Shells vary from the leathery carapace of the softshell turtles to the thick casing of the box turtles, which can make up to a third of the total body weight. The shell is derived from bony plates in the skin which have become fused to the rib cage, and the internal anatomy of the turtle (particularly the limb girdles) has been heavily modified to accommodate the shell.

Like all reptiles, turtles are ectotherms, meaning that they cannot produce their own body heat and must depend upon environmental heat sources. Therefore, turtles spend a large portion of their time basking in the sun, not only to warm their bodies to their optimum temperature, but also to absorb the ultraviolet light, which is necessary for the manufacture of the vitamin D3, used to produce the turtle's shell.

All turtles are amniotes, meaning that they are capable of laying shelled eggs that can develop and hatch on dry land.

Eyes

Turtles have excellent vision and can detect motion at a considerable distance. They can also detect the outlines of potential predators, even if the intruder is perfectly still. Along with their keen sense of smell, turtles use their eyesight as the primary method of finding food. They can see in color and are particularly sensitive to reds and yellows (turtles can also sense a range of infrared wavelengths that are invisible to humans).

Turtle eyes are equipped with two large tear ducts, and in some turtles, these lachrymal glands are used to excrete excess salt from the body.

Skull

As anapsids, turtles lack the spaces between skull bones (called "fossae") that other reptiles possess. These fossae serve as conduits through which the jaw muscles are attached. Turtles, in contrast, have skulls that bulge out at the temporal region to provide attachment places for their muscles.

All turtles lack teeth—they have been replaced by a sharp-edged horny jaw sheath that sometimes has tooth-like serrations. Because they cannot chew, turtles must feed by tearing off bite-sized chunks of food, using their front claws and their powerful jaws, and swallowing food whole.

Tongue

Turtles, like snakes and lizards, possess a Jacobson's organ in the

HELP HERPS

Be wary of capturing your own pets. Not only can wild herps infect your collection with diseases, ticks and mites, but many herps are protected by the federal Endangered Species Act—and you may be breaking the law. It is always best to purchase your herps from a reputable dealer. When you do so, be sure to ask for appropriate documentation showing that your herp was obtained legally.

roof of their mouth. Even though they cannot extend the tongue like snakes do, they use it to capture scent particles in the air and transfer these to the Jacobson's organ. Turtles thus have a keen sense of smell, even underwater.

In many turtles, the tongue is thick and immovable, and cannot be used for swallowing in the normal manner. These turtles can only swallow underwater, where they can use the rush of water to push their food down their throats.

Lungs

Because the shell prevents the chest from expanding, turtles must use a special set of muscles in the body to expand and contract the size of their chest cavity, pumping air in and out of the lungs like a bellows. In addition, many turtles use "gular pumping," in which the throat is expanded to draw in air, that is then pushed down into the lungs. Some turtles are also capable of using the lining of the throat and cloaca to extract oxygen from either air or water. During hibernation, turtles depend completely upon gular pumping and cloacal breathing.

Heart

Like all reptiles (with the exception of the crocodilians), turtles have a three-chambered heart consisting of two atria and a ventricle, which is incompletely divided by a muscular wall. This arrangement allows unoxygenated blood returning from the body to mix with the oxygenated blood returning from the lungs before it is passed on to the rest of the body. Because of this inefficient method of distributing oxygen, turtles tire easily and cannot sustain their activity for long periods of time without frequent stops to rest.

Scutes

Turtle scutes are made up of the protein keratin, the same substance from which human fingernails and hair are made. The scutes are living tissue and contain nerve endings (and turtles can feel it if something is touching their shells). The scutes do not have a large number of pain receptors, but if they are injured or damaged, they have remarkable regenerative powers. The rings which are visible on the scutes of some turtles represent alternate periods of growth and nongrowth, and can be used to roughly estimate the age of the turtle.

Plastron

The bottom portion of the turtle's shell, known as the plastron, is made up of four pairs of bony plates covered with keratin scutes. In some species of turtle, the plastron

A box turtle folds itself into its shell.

is traversed by one or two flexible hinges that allow the turtle to fold its shell and enclose itself tightly within. The plastron is not dragged on the ground when the turtle is walking but is lifted clear by the legs. The plastron scutes are constantly being replaced as they wear off. Some turtles have gaps or openings in the bony plates of the plastron and carapace called "fontanelles," which make the shell lighter.

Carapace

The bony plates that make up the turtle's carapace develop from platelets in the skin called "ossicles" that have become fused to the rib cage and backbone. The shell is therefore permanently attached to the turtle's skeleton, and a living turtle cannot be removed from its shell. The bony plates of the carapace do not coincide with the keratin scutes, which overlay them, and injured turtles that are missing scutes often show a bony seam underneath. The once-common practice of painting the shells of turtles can kill the scutes and infect the underlying bone, causing severe injury.

Pelvic Girdle

Although they have the sprawling gait typical of reptiles, turtles are unique among vertebrates. In all other vertebrates, the bones of the limb girdles are attached to the outside of the rib cage. In turtles, however, the outside of the rib cage has become fused to the bony plates of the carapace, causing the bones of the limb girdles to migrate inside the rib cage. This arrangement produces a limit on the mobility of the turtle's limbs; however, because the turtle is not dependent upon speed for protection, this is not a severe handicap.

Cloaca

The cloaca is the common opening for the turtle's digestive, urinary and reproductive tracts. Like most reptiles, turtles excrete wastes in the form of dry uric acid crystals rather than water-soluble urine.

Turtles practice internal fertilization, in which the sperm is introduced directly into the female's cloaca by the male. Unlike snakes or lizards, turtles do not have hemipenes, but have a single penis. Female turtles are capable of storing live sperm for periods of up to three years after breeding.

Diseases
Salmonella

Salmonella is a potential problem for the turtle's owner, not the reptile. Many species of the *Salmonella* bacteria are capable of infecting the human digestive tract, where they produce severe symptoms including vomiting, cramps, fever and diarrhea. The bacteria readily invade improperly cooked food, (especially poultry and eggs), and they are one of the leading causes of food poisoning.

Several *Salmonella* species, however, are also commonly found inhabiting the skin and digestive tract of reptiles, including turtles, lizards (particularly iguanas) and snakes. Under natural conditions, the population of this organism never builds up to a level where it can produce infections, and most snakes, even those that are carriers of the *Salmonella* organism, show no symptoms of disease. In captivity, however, particularly where the cage is not being kept properly cleaned, *Salmonella* bacteria can be present in high levels in the reptile's feces, its skin, its shed skin or its water.

Although the vast majority of human Salmonella cases are the result of improper food preparation and handling, the medical community has noted a small but disturbing number of *Salmonella* infections that can be directly traced to captive reptiles. Probably the most common method of infection is handling a turtle or the contents of its cage and then placing contaminated fingers into the mouth or eyes. The bacteria can also enter through any small cuts or scratches in the skin. In addition, *Salmonella* organisms can live for several weeks on exposed surfaces, and infections can also occur from contact with areas that have been recently touched or contaminated by a bacteria-carrying reptile. Among those most vulnerable to the disease are small children, pregnant women and those who have suppressed immune systems due to disease or medication. These high-risk people should avoid any direct or indirect contact with captive reptiles.

Fortunately, a few simple precautions can virtually eliminate the danger of contracting a *Salmonella* infection from a captive reptile. First, always wash your hands after handling any reptile or anything from a reptile's cage. Although washing with plain water is ineffective, soap kills the *Salmonella* organism. Second, be sure that your turtle's cage is kept clean, that feces are removed promptly and that the water is changed often. Third, never allow a reptile to come in contact with any surface that is used for human food preparation, such as kitchen counters, sinks or food dishes, and make sure that you wash your hands before touching any such surfaces yourself. Fourth, always supervise small children when they are near the reptiles. Do not let them put their fingers in their mouths while handling the turtle, and make sure they wash their hands promptly afterwards. If these simple rules are followed, it is unlikely that you will ever have any *Salmonella* problems with your reptiles.

Always wash your hands promptly and thoroughly with soap and water after handling a reptile or anything in a reptile's cage.

Incidents of *Salmonella* infection from captive reptiles have not escaped the notice of state and Federal authorities. In 1975, the Federal government passed laws banning the sale of any turtle with a shell length less than four inches, due to outbreaks of *Salmonella* infection that resulted from small children putting turtles in their mouths. It is incumbent upon every responsible reptile keeper to help distribute the information and knowledge necessary to prevent the spread of reptile-borne *Salmonella* before public health officials and legislatures are forced to respond with a new series of legal restrictions on reptile keepers.

Wounds

Minor wounds and scrapes can be treated by dabbing some triple antibiotic cream such as Neosporin, which can be found in any drugstore, onto the injury. Turtles, like most reptiles, have very good internal healing mechanisms, and most minor injuries will heal themselves in a short time.

If the turtle is not housed properly, it can receive minor burns from a heat lamp or sizzle stone. These injuries can also be treated with antibiotic cream.

Creams such as Neosporin, however, are not much use with aquatic turtles, as they are quickly washed off. Aquatic turtles that have suffered a minor wound or injury should be soaked in a separate tank containing a liquid solution of antibiotic such as Betadine, which can usually be found at drugstores. A ten-minute soaking twice a day is sufficient for most minor injuries. The turtle should be rinsed off before being returned to its home tank.

Respiratory Infections

The signs of a respiratory infection are runny eyes, discharge from the nose, gasping or wheezing breaths, and breathing with the mouth open. This problem is nearly always the result of cold or drafty environmental conditions. Turtles from desert or tropical regions can develop colds if they are chilled for even a very short period of time.

Untreated, the infection can spread to the lungs and cause a fatal case of pneumonia.

If the infection is not severe, it can usually be cured by raising the temperature in the turtle's tank by 5 to 10 degrees for a few days. If the symptoms persist, or if the turtle begins having noticeable difficulty in breathing, then it's time for a trip to the veterinarian. Most respiratory infections are treated with antiobiotic injections. Your vet will give you a supply of needles and show you how to administer the shots. The treatment usually lasts two or three weeks.

Intestinal Infections

There is no mistaking the symptoms of an intestinal infection. The turtle will void smelly, slimy feces that are watery and loose. Aquatic turtles will quickly turn their tank into a cesspool, while terrestrial turtles will have you working overtime cleaning their substrate.

There are two possible culprits, and it usually takes a veterinarian to determine which is the cause. One possibility is that *Salmonella* organisms may have built up in the cage to such levels that they have infected the turtle. (This is a certain sign that the tank has not been properly maintained.) Another possibility is that protozoans have infected the turtle's intestinal lining.

Whatever the cause, intestinal troubles can kill a turtle quickly. If you suspect an intestinal infection, get your turtle to a veterinarian immediately for a culture and treatment.

Internal and External Parasites

Parasites are not usually found in captive-bred turtles but are fairly common in wild-caught individuals (especially imports). Because many turtles live in water, and much of their food consists of aquatic prey such as fish, worms and snails, they are more susceptible to parasites than terrestrial turtles.

The most common external parasites on turtles are leeches, which resemble small dark worms that have attached themselves to the turtle's skin. They live by sucking blood from their host, and although they are not often found on terrestrial turtles, they are not uncommon on wild-caught aquatic species.

The best treatment is to carefully remove the leech with a pair of tweezers and then wipe the area with an antiobiotic.

A number of internal parasites can also infest captive turtles. The most common are probably liver flukes, which are found in snails and are passed on to the snail-eating turtle. Nearly every wild-caught aquatic turtle will carry a load of flukes. Usually they are not harmful, but very heavy infestations can destroy the internal organs and kill your turtle. The symptoms are lack of appetite and rapid weight loss.

Severe infestations must be treated by a veterinarian.

If your turtle seems to be eating but not gaining any weight, it may be infested with intestinal worms. Wild turtles are regularly exposed to these parasites, and virtually any wild-caught turtle (and many captive-bred as well) will carry a significant load of worms.

Most intestinal worms that attack turtles have complex life cycles, portions of which are spent inside snails, fish or larger worms. Usually the parasite eggs are passed in the infected turtle's feces and are ingested by snails or other hosts where they hatch. The young parasites are then swallowed by the turtle along with its food, entering the reptile's digestive tract to start the process all over again.

Even if your turtle is captive-bred and was never exposed to the wild, it can still be infected through contaminated food. For this reason, both wild-caught and captive-bred turtles must be examined regularly for the presence of worms or parasites. It is sometimes possible to see dead worms in the turtle's droppings—they look like thin pieces of thread.

The parasites can weaken the turtle by robbing it of nutrients. Heavy infestations can damage the intestines or other internal organs. If you suspect that your turtle has worms, you must take a fresh fecal sample to your veterinarian and have it examined. Intestinal worms can be treated with a dewormer, which is usually given as oral drops or slipped to the turtle in its food.

Cloacal Prolapse

Prolapses occur when the lining of the cloaca protrudes from the anal opening and is exposed outside the body. In some cases, part of the small intestine may also be exposed, and in female turtles, the ovaries may be extended. Although prolapses are horrifying to look at, they are not usually life-threatening to the turtle. The cause of cloacal prolapses is not known—stress and/or the presence of intestinal worms may be involved.

If your turtle suffers a prolapse, it is very important to keep the protruding organs moist. With an aquatic turtle, of course, this presents no problems. Terrestrial turtles, however, should be placed in a bowl of shallow water to keep the organs damp. If the prolapsed tissues dry out, they will die, and it will become necessary for a veterinarian to remove the dead tissues surgically.

Usually, if the turtle is enticed to move around a bit, the prolapse will work itself back in. If necessary, you can gently massage the areas surrounding the protrusion, but you should never attempt to push or force the organs back in. Most often, the prolapse will correct itself in a few days. If it doesn't, it's time to see the veterinarian.

It is also important to ensure that the turtle does not interfere with the prolapse by clawing at it. The reptile is unable to recognize that the prolapse is a part of its own body and may make an effort to detach the "foreign object" from its tail. In addition, other turtles in the tank may attack the prolapse. If a turtle is able to reach the tissue, he will turn it into a bloody mess in a short time. If that happens, surgery will probably be necessary. Although cloacal prolapses are not very common, some individual turtles seem to be prone to them and may experience several prolapses within a short time. In this case your veterinarian can stitch the cloacal opening to make it tighter and prevent further incidents.

Visceral Gout

Visceral gout is a dietary disease that is usually produced by food that is too high in fat. Like most reptiles, turtles cannot digest animal fats very efficiently, and a steady diet of fatty food can cause uric acid crystals to build up in the kidneys and other internal organs. This causes the organs to become rock-hard and stop functioning, which can lead to a very sudden death.

The disease can be prevented by a proper diet and by limiting the intake of animal fats. If you are feeding your turtles canned dog food, make sure that these are made largely with lean meats, such as fish or chicken.

Algae

After a time, your aquatic turtle may begin to sport a rather unattractive coating of green slime, which may also begin to cover the inside of the tank and other exposed surfaces. This is algae, and it is completely harmless to the turtle. Slower-moving aquatic turtles, like snappers, often grow a thick coating of algae to serve as camouflage for their ambush style of hunting.

It is not uncommon for an aquatic turtle to develop a coating of algae on its shell.

A buildup of algae in the tank should not be treated with commercial algicides, as most of these contain hydrochloric acid which can be harmful to the turtles. The best treatment is to periodically change a portion of the water (which should be done as a matter of routine anyway) and to reduce the daily light period by an hour or two.

Fungus

If, instead of slimy green splotches, you begin to see cottony white tufts on the turtle's shell or skin, this is fungus, and it usually attacks the turtle at a point where the skin or shell has been injured. Because most turtles prefer warm damp conditions that favor fungal growth, fungal spores are always present and waiting for an opportunity to invade.

If the fungus gets beneath the scutes, it can penetrate the shell and produce large gaping holes, a condition known as ulcerative shell disease. Eventually the fungus will enter the body cavity, which will be fatal to the turtle.

Fortunately, fungal infections are not difficult to treat. The best remedy is to place the infected turtle in a weak solution of iodine for a ten-minute soak twice a day. Between treatments, keep the turtle dry and maintain a slightly higher temperature in its environment.

To prevent fungal infections, make sure the turtle has a warm and dry basking spot where it can dry off completely. Even in aquatic tanks, the land area must be kept bone dry.

Nutritional Problems

Poor nutrition is probably the most common problem facing captive turtles. Swollen eyes are often caused by a lack of Vitamin A in the diet. It is not a serious disorder if treated promptly. Medicated eye drops are available commercially, and if necessary, a veterinarian can give Vitamin A shots to correct the condition. The diet must be corrected to contain leafy green vegetables, which are high in vitamin A. Carnivorous turtles can be dosed with vitamins by occasionally placing a few drops of cod liver oil on their food.

Young turtles are vulnerable to calcium deficiencies in the diet, which produce soft rubbery shells and deformed limbs. This condition can also be brought on by a lack of proper ultraviolet light. Turtles, like most reptiles, use the ultraviolet wavelengths in natural sunlight to manufacture Vitamin D3 in their skin, which is necessary for utilizing the calcium content of the turtle's food to produce new bone tissue. If the turtle does not receive sufficient UV light or calcium in the diet, it will drain the necessary calcium from its own bones and shell, producing deformities and internal damage.

Treatment consists of calcium supplements added to the food and increased amounts of ultraviolet light.

Species Descriptions
Alligator Snapping Turtle (Macroclemys temmincki)

Level: Advanced
Size: Extra Large
Habitat: Tropical, Aquatic

Biology

The alligator snapping turtle is the largest turtle in North America and, except for the marine turtles, the largest acquatic turtle in the world. Adult turtles can reach a shell length of two and one-half feet and weigh over 250 pounds—unconfirmed reports have put their maximum weight at over 400 pounds. They are so strong that they can carry an adult human being on their shells. Young alligator snappers look much like common snapping turtles but can be distinguished by the extra row of scutes near the margins of the carapace. Like the common snapper, the alligator snapper is incapable of withdrawing its head into its shell.

Despite their large size and fearsome appearance, alligator snappers are not usually aggressive, although large specimens can give a dangerous bite and should not be handled. Alligator snappers have lived almost sixty years in captivity.

When this alligator snapper comes of age, it will be able to give a dangerous bite.

Housing

Although alligator snapping turtles are not very active and do not move around much, the sheer size of the adults requires an extensive tank in which to house them. Although young turtles can be successfully kept in the home, large adults can only be kept in zoos and public aquariums.

Alligator snappers are entirely aquatic and never leave the water except to lay eggs. They are sedentary creatures and spend most of their time quietly resting on the bottom. The water in their tanks should be deep enough so they can just crane their noses to the surface to breathe. Alligator snappers often become covered with algae and other plant growth, providing them with a very effective camouflage as they lie in wait for prey.

They are messy eaters, and alligator snapper tanks require a large efficient filtration system.

Feeding

Alligator snapping turtles feed largely on fish, which they capture by ambush. When hungry, the alligator snapper will lie still on the bottom and open its mouth to display a pink wriggling structure on its tongue. This lure is used to attract fish, which take it for a worm and move closer to investigate. Once the prey is in range, the alligator snapper snaps its jaws shut, spearing the fish with the large hook on its upper jaw and holding it securely.

Breeding

Alligator snapping turtles are only rarely bred in captivity, as breeding would require a huge tank to accommodate an adult breeding pair. In the wild, mating takes place in February and April, and the spherical eggs, which look and feel like Ping-Pong balls, are laid about two months later. The two-inch hatchlings emerge in late summer.

Eastern Box Turtle (Terrapene carolina carolina)

Level: Novice
Size: Medium
Habitat: Temperate, Terrestrial

Biology

Although they are the best-known of the terrestrial turtles, eastern box turtles are actually members of the emydid family and are closely related to the aquatic sliders and painted turtles.

The most obvious feature of the eastern box turtle is its closable shell. When threatened, the turtle is able to pull its head and legs into its shell and close it tightly. The turtle can stay closed up for several hours before it must extend its head to breathe.

Box turtles have one of the longest life spans of any living animal and have been known to live for over 125 years. Several subspecies of box turtle are available in the pet trade, including the Gulf Coast box turtle, the Florida box turtle and the three toed box turtle. In many areas, box turtle populations are declining due to habitat loss and overcollection for the pet trade. They have recently been added to the list of threatened species and a permit is required to capture them. Make sure that any box turtles you keep as pets have been captive-bred.

Housing

Eastern box turtles are largely terrestrial but do spend some time in the water. They require large cages with a lot of room for wandering, and a shallow water dish big enough for them to climb into. Like all turtles, they require access to unfiltered ultraviolet light. Hibernating turtles will bury themselves in leaf litter or mud, but they can be kept active throughout the winter if suitable temperatures are maintained. Like all turtles, though, they must be hibernated if breeding is to be successful.

Eastern box turtles are somewhat territorial, particularly the males, and if several turtles are kept together they may snap at each other to establish dominance. In the wild, an eastern box turtle rarely travels more than about 700 feet away from its home area.

Feeding

Like most of its emydid relatives, the eastern box turtle is largely carnivorous when young, becoming more and more herbivorous with age. In the wild, they eat earthworms, snails, salamanders, berries and plants. They will also eat such lethal mushrooms as the Death Angel, to which they are immune. Captives do well on a diet of canned dog food to which a calcium supplement powder has been added. They will also eat raspberries, bananas, peanut butter and green leafy vegetables.

Captive box turtles tend toward obesity and should be fed only every other day. If overfed, they will soon become so fat that they can't close both halves of their shells at the same time.

Breeding

Male eastern box turtles can be recognized by the shallow depression in the rear portion of their plastron. Males also tend to have red eyes, while females tend to have brown eyes. Breeding takes place in the spring, after a mating ritual during which the male repeatedly bites the female along the carapace.

Several weeks later, the female will excavate a nest in mud or sand and lay up to ten soft oval eggs. These hatch in about three months. Hatchling box turtles are about one and one-half inches long and have rounded shells. They reach sexual maturity in about twelve years, at a shell length of about five inches. Female box turtles are still capable of laying eggs at the age of fifty-five years.

Florida Softshell Turtle (Apalone ferox)

Level: Intermediate
Size: Large
Habitat: Tropical, Aquatic

Biology

There are a number of different species of softshell turtles, forming a very widespread family of turtles. Fossil softshell turtles have been found as far back as the middle Cretaceous period during the time of the dinosaurs.

The male eastern box turtle generally has red eyes.

Softshells are large, aggressive aquatic reptiles. At a shell length of over eighteen inches, they are bigger than the snapping turtles and just as mean. Because they have light, soft, pliable shells, softshells are fast and active, and their speed, combined with their sharp jaws and long necks, makes them difficult to handle safely.

The species most commonly encountered in the pet trade are the Florida softshell, the smooth softshell and the spiny softshell. The care of all of these turtles is similar. Softshell turtles are used as food in localities where they are common. In China and Japan, they are considered a delicacy. Captive softshell turtles can live up to twenty-five years.

Florida softshell turtles prefer shallow pools with sandy bottoms (albino).

Housing

Florida softshell turtles can be found in nearly any permanent body of water except for areas with rapids, but they prefer shallow pools with soft sandy bottoms. Although they are excellent swimmers, they tend to avoid deep water and prefer to rest on the bottom in shallow areas, buried in the sand, where they can extend their long necks and breathe through their snorkel-like nose. While underwater, they can also breathe by pumping water in and out of their throats, where a large number of tiny fingerlike projections help absorb oxygen.

Captive softshell turtles require large shallow tanks. They are capable of living in a purely aquatic tank with no land area, but prefer to leave the water occasionally. They do not often bask but will float just beneath the surface with the top of their shell exposed to the sun.

Feeding

Although softshell turtles are aquatic feeders and must be underwater to swallow their food, they only rarely eat fish in the wild. The primary food of the Florida softshell is aquatic snails, which they crush with their wide flat jaws. Softshells will also eat frogs, tadpoles, worms and crayfish. Captives can usually be taught to accept whole fish or pieces of lean beef or liver. Whole prey is best from a nutritional point of view. Softshell

turtles will also attempt to eat smaller turtles and must be kept in a species-specific tank with individuals of their own size.

Breeding

Softshell turtles nest in the spring, laying up to twenty-five hard white spherical eggs in depressions scooped out of sandy shorelines. The eggs are relatively smaller than most turtle eggs—about one inch wide—and resemble Ping-Pong balls. In warm areas, females may lay up to five clutches of eggs per year. They hatch in about two months. Newly emerged turtles are about one and one-half inches long.

Unlike most turtles, softshell turtle eggs are not temperature-influenced for sex. For some reason, softshell turtles also seem to be more likely to produce albinos than are other turtles.

Greek Tortoise
(Testudo hermanni)

Level: Intermediate
Size: Medium
Habitat: Savannah, Terrestrial

Biology

The Greek tortoise, also known as the Hermann's tortoise, is native to the southern parts of Europe near the Mediterranean, from Spain to Turkey. It prefers a dry habitat including oak forests and hillsides. It should not be confused with the Mediterranean spur thighed tortoise, which, despite the Latin name Testudo graeca, is not found in Greece.

A medium-sized tortoise, the Greek tortoise reaches a shell length of about eight inches. It is threatened or endangered throughout most of its range, due to habitat loss and overcollection for the pet trade. Its export is now legally protected by the CITES treaty.

Housing

Accomodations for a Greek tortoise must be warm and dry. Daytime temperatures in the low 80s are suitable, dropping to the mid-70s at night. The cage should be relatively large to allow the turtles to wander around and get exercise.

Feeding

Like most tortoises, Greek tortoises are largely herbivorous and feed on fruit, greens and flowers. Younger individuals also take some meat, and will accept worms, snails and insects.

Although they are native to dry areas, Greek tortoises must be provided with drinking water at all times.

Breeding

Male Greek tortoises may be distinguished from females by the concave depression on their plastron and their longer tail. The tortoises take as long as ten to fifteen years to reach breeding age.

During the breeding season, male turtles may challenge each other by butting shells. During mating, the male uses a horny clawlike tip on his tail to stimulate the female.

Up to a dozen eggs are laid in an excavated nest, and these hatch in about three months. In a suitable habitat, several clutches may be laid each year.

Hingeback Tortoise
(Kinixys belliana)

Level: Intermediate
Size: Medium
Habitat: Savannah, Terrestrial

Biology

Hingeback tortoises are native to the arid southern parts of Africa. The most widely available species, the Bell's hingeback tortoise, is found in the dry arid regions of northern Madagascar and on nearby areas of the mainland.

Hingebacks tortoises can encase themselves in their shells like box turtles (Home's hingeback tortoise).

The Bell's hingeback tortoise is the most widely available of the hingebacks.

Although they can close themselves into their shells like box turtles, these two species are not closely related. The hingeback tortoise's shell closes along a single hinge which runs across the rear third of the carapace. This allows the rear of the carapace to be pulled in over the back legs and tail.

Hingeback tortoises reach a shell length of about eight inches.

Housing
Hingeback tortoises are native to dry arid regions, where they seek shelter near water holes and other damp areas. They require high temperatures and strong light. If the temperature is maintained in the 80s, they can be given the free run of a room. They must be provided with a source of ultraviolet light and a shallow pan of water for drinking and occasional soaking. In captivity, they must be provided with a high humidity.

Feeding
Hingeback tortoises are omnivorous but tend to eat more plant material than animal food. They can be fed melons, berries and leafy green vegetables such as kale or endive. Young turtles will also eat earthworms and insects.

As an adaptation to living in arid semi-desert areas, hingeback tortoises have large anal sacks that are capable of storing water for long periods of time. In a fully loaded turtle, these sacks may take up over half the body cavity. African natives who live in these areas often dig up estivating turtles (turtles in a dormant state caused by the dryness of summer conditions) and puncture them to drain out the water.

Breeding
Hingeback tortoises lay their eggs in shallow nests scooped out in sandy areas. The hatchlings are boldly patterned, but these bright colors tend to fade as the turtle gets older. Young hingebacks do not have functional hinges—the hinge becomes moveable only when the turtle is several years old.

Leopard Tortoise (Geochelone pardalis)

Level: Intermediate
Size: Large
Habitat: Savannah, Terrestrial

Biology
The leopard tortoise is native to the hot dry savannahs of East Africa. They are members of the Testudo family, which contains about fifty species of terrestrial turtles, most of them from Africa and Madagascar. Large numbers of leopard tortoises were once exported from Africa for the pet trade with most of the exportation going to Europe. This overcollection has drastically reduced the native populations, and most Testudo turtles are now protected as threatened species. Those available in the pet trade have been captive-bred.

A young leopard tortoise may take as long as twenty-five years to reach sexual maturity.

The leopard tortoise reaches a shell length of eighteen inches and can weigh as much as fifty pounds. Captives have lived for as long as seventy-five years.

Housing

Leopard tortoises are large and active, requiring spacious cages with high temperatures and strong lighting. They can usually be given the free run of the house as long as they have a source of ultraviolet light for basking and a water dish for drinking. In warm areas, they can also be kept in outdoor enclosures which include dry sandy areas with some low plants to provide shade.

Feeding

Leopard tortoises are largely herbivorous and will eat leafy green vegetation, melons, berries and fruits. Young specimens will take earthworms and other invertebrates and must be provided with calcium supplements. Although they are desert animals, leopard tortoises need periodic access to water, which they will store inside their bodies.

Breeding

Leopard tortoises require large spacious outdoor enclosures for successful breeding. The males can be recognized by the concave depression in the rear half of their plastrons. During warm weather, the male will pursue the females continuously until they allow him to mate.

Up to a dozen eggs are laid in a nest dug out by the female in a sandy, dry area. The eggs hatch in about three months, and usually, captive-bred eggs must be artificially incubated. The hatchlings must be kept warm and dry, and must be provided with calcium supplements to ensure proper shell growth. They grow very slowly and may take as long as twenty years to reach sexual maturity.

Mud Turtle
(Kinosternon subrubrum)

Level: Novice
Size: Small
Habitat: Temperate, Aquatic

Biology

Mud turtles are the most aquatic of turtles and never leave the water except to lay eggs. They are closely related to the musk turtles and have a similar appearance, but they can be distinguished by the triangular pectoral scutes on the plastron—these are rectangular in the musk turtles. Mud turtles rarely exceed five inches in length.

There are about fifteen species of mud turtle, but several, including the eastern mud turtle, have been greatly reduced in population because of habitat loss. The most commonly available species are the Florida mud turtle and the Mississippi mud turtle. All of these species can be cared for in the same manner. Mud turtles have been known to live up to thirty-eight years in captivity.

Housing

Mud turtles are one of the few reptiles that can live comfortably in a totally aquatic aquarium with no land area to crawl out onto. They prefer shallow, slow-moving water with a soft muddy bottom but will do well in an aquarium with an underwater rock cave to serve as a retreat. No substrate is necessary. Unlike the related musk turtles, mud turtles can tolerate somewhat salty or brackish water. They do not usually bask but often float just below the surface with their shells protruding.

Feeding

Mud turtles feed largely on carrion and small aquatic invertebrates, as well as a small amount of plant food. Captives should be fed whole goldfish or minnows, supplemented with trout pellets, earthworms and snails. Small specimens of the mud turtle are prone to calcium deficiencies.

Breeding

Male mud turtles are unusual among turtles in possessing a rough, dark patch of skin on the rear legs, which grip the female during mating. Only mud turtles and the closely related musk turtles possess these pads. Mud turtles breed in the spring and lay two to four eggs per clutch. They may, on occasion, lay two clutches in a single year. The females seem to be only half-hearted about their eggs, often leaving them only half-buried or sometimes even lying out in the open. Enough of the eggs survive, however, to keep the population from dwindling. Mud turtles reach sexual maturity at an age of five to seven years.

Musk Turtle (Sternotherus odoratus)

Level: Novice
Size: Small
Habitat: Temperate, Aquatic

Biology

At an average length of just four inches, the musk turtle is the smallest turtle in North America and one of the smallest in the world. Despite their small size, however, they are pugnacious little creatures and are prone to bite. With their long necks, they can reach almost as far back as their hind legs to bite a handler. Another defense is the foul-smelling oil produced by two scent glands under the carapace, which have earned these little turtles the name "stinkpot."

Musk turtles are largely nocturnal. They are unique among turtles in having a prehensile tail, which is capable of grasping objects. This, combined with the great mobility of their legs, makes them excellent climbers, and musk turtles have been found in tree branches as far as six feet from the ground. They will drop into the water at the slightest disturbance. Captive musk turtles have lived as long as twenty-three years.

Housing

In the wild, musk turtles prefer stagnant, shallow water with a thick, muddy bottom. In captivity, such a substrate would make an intolerable mess, and they are best kept in a bare tank with no substrate. Musk turtles are very insecure and will not do well unless they are provided with an underwater cave to use

It can be hard to reconcile the nastiness of the musk turtle's odor with its tiny size (loggerhead musk turtle).

as a hiding place. They are almost completely aquatic and rarely leave the water. Instead of basking on shore like most other turtles, musk turtles prefer to float with their shells just below the water surface. Captive musk turtles do not require any land area in their tanks, but the water should be shallow enough for them to extend their nose to the surface to breathe. They are not very good swimmers and move about by walking along the bottom.

In the winter, several dozen musk turtles may congregate in a patch of mud to hibernate, but they can be kept active throughout the winter if kept at room temperature.

Feeding

Approximately half of the musk turtle's diet consists of dead fish and other scavenged carrion. They will also eat tadpoles, frog eggs, snails and worms, and are often mistakenly caught by fishermen when they try to rob bait from the hook. In captivity, they can be fed earthworms, trout pellets, small pieces of beef and liver, and whole fish such as minnows or goldfish. Because the turtles are not fast enough to catch live fish, the fish should be pre-killed before feeding.

Breeding

Female musk turtles can be recognized by a row of warty projections that run along the spine of their tail. Male musk turtles have much wider patches of skin between the plastron scutes than do females. During the breeding season, males also develop a rough patch of skin on the inner thighs to help hold the female during mating. These structures are similar to the nuptial pads of male frogs. In turtles, they are only found in the mud turtle and musk turtle.

The eggs of musk turtles are hard and brittle, similar to bird eggs, and they hatch in two or three months. There are usually two clutches per year with two to four eggs per clutch. Rather than digging a nest for their eggs, musk turtles lay their eggs half-buried in leaf litter, or sometimes right out in the open. It is not unusual for several females to choose the same spot to lay their eggs. The hatchling turtles are less than one inch long.

The males reach sexual maturity at an age of three years, while the larger females cannot breed until they are nine or ten years old.

Ornate Box Turtle (Terrapene ornata)

Level: Novice
Size: Medium
Habitat: Savannah, Terrestrial

Biology

The ornate box turtle is probably the most widely kept of all the box turtles, even though it is listed as a threatened species in the wild. Although it is closely related to the eastern box turtle, it is a separate species which has become specialized for a different habitat. The ornate box turtle is native to the prairies and grasslands of the central

A threatened species in the wild, the ornate box turtle is a popular pet.

United States and rarely enters the kind of woodland habitat favored by the eastern species. It can be distinguished from the various subspecies of the eastern box turtle by its lack of a longitudinal keel on the carapace and by the striking radiated pattern on its plastron. The ornate box turtle also tends to be somewhat smaller in size than its eastern cousin.

Like all box turtles, it is capable of drawing itself tightly into its shell and can have a life span of over 100 years. The ornate box turtle is diurnal but tends to spend the hottest parts of the day in the shade of its burrow.

The eggs of a ornate box turtle will hatch in approximately three months.

Housing

Because ornate box turtles are adapted to the American prairies, they can tolerate much hotter and drier conditions than the eastern box turtle. They do, however, require access to water for drinking and soaking, and a shallow water pan should be provided in their cage. They also need a source of ultraviolet light, such as a sunlamp or unfiltered sunlight. Captives do best if they are allowed to roam outside for several hours a week. They can also be given the free run of a room, as long as they have a basking spot and a water pan available to them.

In the colder areas of their range, ornate box turtles will burrow into the ground at the first sign of cold weather, burrowing deeper to hibernate as winter sets in. Captives can be kept active all winter if the temperature is kept above 75 degrees.

Feeding

In keeping with its habitat, the ornate box turtle is much more carnivorous than most other box turtles. In the wild, most of its diet consists of grasshoppers and beetles. It will also eat carrion and occasionally fallen fruit. Captives will eat crickets and can also be fed canned cat food. They will occasionally eat food such as melons, bananas or berries.

Breeding

Although the ornate box turtle is similar in appearance and habits to the eastern box turtle, they are different species and do not normally interbreed. The ornate box turtle lays eggs in early summer in a shallow nest that the female excavates with her back feet. Two to eight eggs are laid, and these hatch in about three months. The hatchlings reach sexual maturity in about eight years.

Painted Turtle
(Chrysemys picta)

Level: Novice
Size: Medium
Habitat: Temperate, Semi-Aquatic

Biology

There are four subspecies of painted turtle found throughout the United States, each brightly colored with splashes of red and yellow on an olive background. Each subspecies prefers its own range of climatic conditions, and together they range from the warm humid areas of Florida to the cold climates of Nova Scotia. Unlike most turtles, which shed their skin in small flakes that are virtually unnoticeable, painted

Painted turtles shed their scutes in large pieces, unlike most turtles that shed in small flakes (southern painted turtle).

turtles shed their scutes in large pieces that peel off the shell.

Laboratory experiments on painted turtles have also shown them to be quite intelligent for a reptile. They are capable of learning to differentiate between various stripe patterns and can remember what they have learned for as long as three months. In captivity, painted turtles have lived up to eleven years.

Housing

Housing requirements for the painted turtle are similar to those for the red eared slider, and these two species can be successfully kept in the same tank. In the wild, painted turtles tend to prefer shallow stagnant water with a soft bottom and lots of basking spots. Painted turtles usually have more than one body of water in their home range and will often travel overland from one to the other. Most subspecies of painted turtle can tolerate lower temperatures than other aquatic turtles, and the eastern races have been observed swimming under the ice in winter time.

Feeding

Like most aquatic turtles, painted turtles are almost entirely carnivorous when young but become progressively more herbivorous as they get older. They hunt largely by smell and can pick up scents underwater by drawing water in through the nose and expelling it from the mouth, allowing it to pass over the Jacobson's organ.

Captive painted turtles can be fed goldfish, earthworms, trout pellets and varying amounts of plant food. Baby painted turtles require calcium supplements, which can most easily be provided by dissolving a piece of chalk or limestone in their tank. Like all aquatic turtles, they must be underwater to swallow food.

Breeding

Painted turtles breed in March and April. Mating takes place in the water with the male using his long front claws to stroke the female. In early summer, the females will wander overland to find a suitable spot for egg-laying. The soft oval eggs are buried about four inches deep in sand or mud. Painted turtles are quite prolific and may lay four or five clutches per year, each containing up to two dozen eggs. The eggs usually hatch in about ninety days, but in cooler areas they may cease their development through the winter and hatch the following spring.

The hatchling turtles are about one inch long and are brightly colored. Male painted turtles reach sexual maturity in two to five years. Females reach maturity two to three years later.

Red Eared Slider
(Trachemys elegans)

Level: Novice
Size: Medium
Habitat: Tropical, Aquatic

Biology

The red eared slider is probably the most widely kept reptile pet in the world, and millions are sold in the pet trade every year. Unfortunately, most of these turtles die from improper care. Although they are native to the southeastern United States, they have been established in many non-native areas through the escape or liberation of pets. Red eared sliders can be recognized by the bright red patch or stripe behind the eyes.

As they get older, red eared sliders tend to get darker in color, and very old specimens, especially males, may be a dull olive green or even black. Properly cared for, red eared sliders can live for as long as seventy-five years.

Housing

Housing for the red eared slider is typical of that for all semi-aquatic turtles. About two thirds of the tank should be filled with water at least as deep as the length of the turtle's carapace. A water temperature of approximately 75 degrees is required. Because these turtles spend much of their time basking, they also require a rock pile or basking platform where they can leave the water and dry off completely. A hot spot must be provided at the basking site.

Like most turtles, red eared sliders require exposure to an amount of ultraviolet light to properly utilize several vitamins. This can be provided either with an artificial sun lamp or access to unfiltered natural sunlight. Red eared sliders will foul their water quickly, and an efficient filtration system is a necessity in their tanks.

Feeding

Red eared sliders feed largely on small fish and aquatic invertebrates. Captives will take goldfish, earthworms and snails, and can also be fed trout pellets and a small amount of plant material. Commercial turtle foods consisting of dried ant pupae lack a number of vital nutritional requirements and should be avoided. Baby turtles are prone to calcium deficiencies, and this can be combatted by dissolving a piece of chalk or limestone in the tank. Because they cannot manipulate their tongue for swallowing, sliders must use a flow of water to push food into their stomachs and therefore can only swallow when underwater.

A good idea is to train your turtles to eat in a separate tank which can be easily emptied and cleaned, so as to avoid fouling the main tank unnecessarily. Uneaten food in the tank can lead to infections and health problems for the turtle keeper as well as the turtle.

Breeding

Red eared sliders can be bred in captivity, but successful breeding usually requires a large outdoor enclosure with an artificial pond. Males can be recognized by the long claws on the front feet and by their smaller size. Mating takes place in the water after a courtship ritual in which the male faces the female and uses his long claws to stroke her face. Up to twelve eggs are laid in a nest dug into mud or sand and carefully camouflaged with vegetation. They hatch in about sixty days.

The red eared slider is easily recognized by the bright red stripe behind its eyes.

The hatchlings are about two inches long and are very brightly colored. The males are ready to breed when they reach a size of three and one-half to four inches, while females reach sexual maturity a few years later, at a size of six to seven inches. Red eared sliders are capable of breeding and laying eggs up to the age of sixty years.

Common Snapping Turtle (Chelydra serpentina)

Level: Intermediate
Size: Large
Habitat: Temperate, Aquatic

Biology

Snappers are one of the most widespread turtles in the world and are found virtually throughout North America. Adult snappers can reach a carapace length of eighteen inches and weigh up to fifty pounds. They have such small plastrons that they can't retract their heads or legs all the way under their shells and are thus vulnerable to predators if they are flipped onto their backs. As a result, they are aggressive and will actively bite and snap to defend themselves with their powerful bulldog jaws. Because they have no aquatic predators, though, they will not usually attempt to bite while they are underwater.

Snapping turtles never become tame and will actively bite—they do not make the best pets (common snapping turtle).

Captive snapping turtles never become tame and can be dangerous to handle. They should always be carried by the back legs, never by the tail. Snappers have lived up to twenty-five years in captivity.

Housing

Snapping turtles are not very active animals and do not require a large amount of room in their tanks. They are completely aquatic and do not require any land area. The water should be deep enough so the snapper can just barely crane his nose to the surface to breathe. Snappers do not require any heaters—they range as far north as Canada and can tolerate colder conditions than most turtles. They are not effective swimmers and move around by simply walking along the bottom.

Because of their sedentary habits, they often become coated with a layer of algae and aquatic vegetation, and look like large rocks resting on the bottom.

In the wild, they can be found in virtually any permanent body of water, even in close proximity to humans. In fact, snapping turtles have been found living in ponds in New York's Central Park.

Feeding

Snapping turtles are voracious feeders and will eat virtually anything that is or once was alive, including fish, smaller turtles and aquatic vegetation. They have also been known to capture birds and small mammals. Captives should be fed whole prey animals, such as rodents and fish, for proper nutrient balance.

Snapping turtles will tear large food items apart with their claws and make a mess of their tank. Accordingly, it is advised to cut their food into bite-sized pieces before feeding. Be very careful when feeding a large snapper; its powerful jaws are quite capable of removing a finger.

Breeding

Because a breeding pair of snappers would require a very large pool of water and lots of space, they are not often bred in captivity. In the wild, breeding takes place in the spring, and the eggs are laid in early summer. The twenty-five to fifty eggs look like little Ping-Pong balls and are so tough that they will actually bounce if dropped. The eggs are often laid a considerable distance from water.

Most snapper eggs hatch in about four months, but in the northern parts of their range, the hatchlings may overwinter in the egg and hatch the following spring.

Snapping turtles, like many reptiles, exhibit temperature-dependent sex determination, in which eggs that incubate at a certain temperature range will always produce males, while those incubated at a different temperature range always produce females. Snappers are unusual, however, in producing female hatchlings at cooler temperatures. Most turtles produce males at lower temperatures.

Spotted Turtle (Clemmys guttata)

Level: Intermediate
Size: Medium
Habitat: Temperate, Semi-Aquatic

Biology

The spotted turtle is native to the northeastern United States where it can be found in bogs, marshes and wet woodlands. The color pattern—black or dark blue with bright yellow spots—serves as camouflage, mimicking its sun-dappled habitat.

At a shell length of around five inches, the spotted turtle is one of the smallest of the *Clemmys* group. Captive individuals have lived over forty years.

Spotted turtles have become rare due to the rapid loss of their habitat. In many states, they are legally protected.

Housing

Spotted turtles are semi-aquatic and prefer to live in ponds, marshes and bogs. They thrive in stagnant or slow-moving water with a muddy bottom. Although they sometimes inhabit large rivers, they avoid the swiftly moving sections and stay in the marshy areas near shore.

In captivity, they can be kept in a semi-terrestrial aquarium with a half-land, half- water area. The water should be at least as deep as the shell length of the turtle. The land area should be covered with moss, leaf litter or some other soft substrate.

Like nearly all turtles, they need a basking spot and a source of ultraviolet light in their tank.

Feeding

Spotted turtles are carnivorous and feed in the wild on aquatic insects, small fish and invertebrates. Captives can be fed crickets, earthworms and goldfish.

Breeding

Although spotted turtles are listed as "threatened" in many states, they are not widely captive bred. Male

The spotted turtle's yellow spots serve as camouflage in its sun-dappled habitat.

turtles usually have brown eyes, while females usually have orange eyes. Breeding occurs in late spring and can take place either in or out of the water. In June, up to eight eggs are laid in a nest excavated by the female. The young hatch about seventy days later. In some cases, the young may overwinter in the egg before hatching the following spring.

Hatchlings are about one inch long and reach sexual maturity in seven to ten years, at a shell length of about four inches.

Wood Turtle
(Clemmys insculpta)

Level: Intermediate
Size: Medium
Habitat: Temperate, Semi-Aquatic

Biology

Wood turtles were once common throughout the damp woodlands of the northeastern United States, but overcollecting for use as food in the 1920s led to declining populations—they are now listed as endangered in several states. Please make sure that any wood turtles you obtain were captive-bred and not taken from the wild.

Often called "old red legs," a reference to the bright orange skin on their legs and throat, wood turtles are the largest member of the *Clemmys* genus in the United States, reaching a shell length of around nine inches. Captive wood turtles have lived to almost sixty years.

Wood turtles are reportedly the most intelligent of the turtles, and often learn to respond to their own names. In laboratory experiments, wood turtles have learned to run mazes nearly as quickly as white rats and can retain this knowledge for several months.

Housing

Wood turtles spend about half of their time in the water and half of it on land, and their accommodations must take these habits into account. The tank should be large, at least the size of a twenty-gallon aquarium, and should be divided into equal land and water areas. The land area should contain a layer of dirt for digging, covered with a moss or leaf litter substrate. The water area should be about half as deep as the shell length.

Wood turtles range as far north as Nova Scotia, and because they can tolerate somewhat cooler temperatures, no heater is required for them.

Feeding

Wood turtles are omnivorous and will eat both plant and animal material, although they tend to eat more vegetable matter as they get older. In the wild, they will eat worms, salamanders, berries and mushrooms. Captives will do well on a diet of canned dog food, supplemented with calcium powder. They will also eat berries and green leafy vegetables, such as mustard greens or dandelion leaves, and fruits such as cantaloupes and apples.

Breeding

Because they are rare and threatened in many areas, some effort is being made to breed wood turtles in captivity. Mating takes place in the spring and always occurs in water. A clutch of six to eight eggs is laid in May or June, and these hatch in early autumn. The emerging hatchlings are about one and one-half inches long.

Hatchling wood turtles are about one and one-half inches in length.

CHAPTER 5

Lizards

Lizards belong to the order Sauria, part of the super-order Squamata that also includes the snakes. There are about 3,000 species of lizards existing today.

Agamids

Consisting of about 300 species, the agamids are predominantly from Africa. In addition to the common agama species, the agamid family also contains the bearded dragons, the calotes lizards and the uromastyx dab lizards. Two unusual members of this family are the moloch or thorny devil, an Australian lizard that protects itself with a fearsome coating of sharp spines, and the flying dragon, a lizard that glides from tree to tree using folds of skin stretched between elongated ribs.

The panther chameleon's amazingly long tongue is used to capture a grasshopper.

Chamaeleoinids

The eighty-five species of "true chameleons" are famous for their ability to alter their color to match their surroundings, but they have many other interesting traits. The tongue, which is used to capture prey, is almost twice as long as the body, while the eyes are set in projecting turrets and can move independently to scan the surroundings for prey. Chameleons are delicate animals and are very difficult to keep in captivity.

Iguanids

A large family that is nearly limited to the western hemisphere (the sole exceptions being a few species on Madagascar), this group contains the various species of iguana and spiny iguana, as well as other genera such as the chuckwalla. Many genera that were formerly included in the iguanids have been broken off into separate families.

Corytophanids

The corytophanid family contains the well-known basilisk lizards. There are two species found in Latin America. Two other closely related genera are also classed with the corytophanids.

Phrynosomatids

Over sixty species of the horned and spiny lizards are found throughout the western United States, including the various species of horned lizards (sometimes

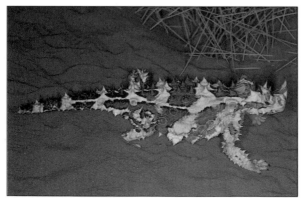

The thorny devil is aptly named.

mistakenly referred to as "horned toads") and spiny lizards, including the blue bellied, the utas and side blotched lizards. The phrynosomids used to be classed with the iguanids but have been reclassified as a separate family.

Crotaphytids

The crotaphytid family is comprised of the collared lizards, with several species ranging throughout the western United States. The collared lizards were formerly classed with the iguanids.

Polychrotids

Among the genera included in this family are the anoles, which were formerly classed with the iguanids. As the name suggests, members of this family have at least a limited

These collared lizards (male, top; female, bottom), make the western U.S. their home.

ability to vary their body color according to mood and temperature. There are over 300 species, mostly in Latin America. Only one species, the green anole, is native to the United States, but several other species have been introduced to this country. The anoles are the largest group of lizards found in the western hemisphere.

Gekkonids

One of the largest and most varied families of lizards, the 750 species of geckos range in size from the tiny Mediterranean gecko to the large tokays. Found in all parts of the world, there are six species in the United States. Nearly all geckos are nocturnal.

Eublepharids

Including the leopard geckos and banded geckos, these lizards were formerly placed in the gekkonid family, but several authorities have advocated placing them in a family of their own.

Pygopodids

The "snake lizards" make up a group of thirty-one species from Australia. All are limbless burrowers. Very little is known about their biology.

Little is known about the mysterious "snake lizards."

Gerrhosaurids

The plated lizards are an African group of seventy skink-like lizards with stiff, bony skins. The gerrhosaurid family also includes the zonures and girdle-tailed lizards.

Teiids

This family includes the various species of tegu as well as the North American whiptails and the ameivas. There are about 225 species found only in the western hemisphere. Only fourteen of these species reach the United States (all are members of the whiptail genus *Cnemidophorus*). The teiids are the only family of lizards to exhibit parthenogenesis, in which females lay eggs without first having mated with a male.

Scincids

A large and diverse family with over 1,200 species, skinks are found in all parts of the world in every conceivable environment. Only one genus, *Eumeces,* is found in the western hemisphere.

The skinks range in size from the small North American five lined skink to the huge prehensile tailed skink and blue tongue skink. In habitat, they are found in temperate forests, tropical jungles and dry arid deserts.

Several of the skinks are limbless and resemble snakes.

Lacertids

This is an Old World family containing around 200 species of "typical lizards," including the European wall lizard and the emerald lacerta. The family ranges from Europe to Asia and Africa. There are no lacertids in Madagascar.

Although not often seen for sale in the United States, this family is popular among European herpers.

Anguids

This family contains the alligator lizards and the various species of glass lizards. The glass lizards are often mistaken for snakes. The anguids are characterized by bony plates in their skin, which give them a stiff feeling.

As a group, the anguids consist of seventy-five species, which are found in North and South America as well as Europe and Africa.

Aniellids

This small family contains two species of legless lizards found in California. These are limbless burrowers and are sometimes grouped with the anguids.

Varanids

The varanid family contains forty species of monitors and goannas. All of the monitors are large and active predators. They fill a number of environmental niches, from the green tree monitor, which is largely arboreal, to the Komodo dragon, a terrestrial predator that is at the top of its food chain. As a group, varanids are

The five lined skink is one of the smaller members of the skink family.

The Mexican beaded lizard (left) and the gila monster (right) are both venomous and are exceptionally poor choices for pets.

found in Africa, Asia and Australia. None are found in the United States.

Lanthonotids

A single-species family containing the Borneo earless monitor. Although related to the varanids, the earless monitor displays many snakelike characteristics. It is a semi-aquatic burrower.

Xantusiids

The "night lizards" are a small family comprised of eighteen species, ranging from the United States to Latin America. Night lizards lack eyelids and are unusual among lizards in bearing live young instead of laying eggs.

Dibamids

All but one of the ten species in this "blind lizard" family are found in Southeast Asia; the lone straggler is found in Mexico. These eyeless burrowers lack front limbs (and sometimes also rear limbs), but little is known about their biology and habits.

Helodermatids

The helodermatids are the only venomous lizards. There are only two species in this family, the Mexican beaded lizard and the gila monster, both found in Mexico and the American Southwest. The venom drains into the base of the lizard's lip and is chewed into the wound by the teeth.

Natural History

Although the name "dinosaur" means "terrible lizards," modern lizards are not actually descended from the Mesozoic dinosaurs, although both groups are diapsids—meaning they have two bony arches in the skull through which the jaw muscles pass.

As a group, reptiles are descendents of amphibians—most likely a group of amphibians known as labrynthodonts. It is not known from which particular group of labrynthodont amphibians the reptiles developed; during the same time frame, several different families of ancient amphibians seem to have been developing characteristics similar to those of reptiles.

The oldest fossil that can be definitely recognized as a reptile is a small lizardlike animal known as *Hylonomus,* whose skeletons have been found inside petrified tree stumps in Nova Scotia. During the period of time in which *Hylonomus* lived, the earth was a different place than it is now. The continents were all joined into one large supercontinent known as Pangea ("all earth"), and even such places as Antarctica and northern Canada had warm, humid climates with lush tropical forests.

Hylonomus was a member of a group of very ancient reptiles known as the cotylosaurs, or "stem reptiles," believed by paleontologists to be ancestral to all of the reptile families alive today. The cotylosaurs first appeared during the Permian period, the period of time that immediately preceded the rise of the dinosaurs. During the next few million years, the cotylosaurs diverged into three distinct groups of reptiles that are distinguished from each other by their differing skull structures. The earliest of the cotylosaurs were anapsids, which means that they lacked any arches or openings between their skull bones. The anapsids eventually went on to produce the modern turtles. Later, another group of cotylosaurs developed a single arch in the skull, between the postorbital and squamosal bones, through which the jaw muscles passed. These reptiles are known as synapsids, and they went on to evolve into the modern mammals. The third group of reptiles, the diapsids, diversified to produce the extinct dinosaurs as well as the modern lizards and snakes.

The earliest recognizable lizard to appear in the fossil record dates from the early Triassic period, about 200 million years ago, and is known as *Prolacerta*.

Another ancient lizard has been found in Jurassic deposits almost 180 million years old. This fossil, known as *Paliguana,* measures about sixteen inches long and was found in South Africa. The fossilized remains of a very large member of the monitor lizard family, known as *Megalania,* have been found in Australia. This lizard, at a length of fifteen feet and a weight of 1,000 pounds, is almost twice as large as the biggest living lizard (the Komodo dragon). *Megalania* went extinct only 10,000 years ago—a very recent period in geological time.

Another extinct lizard, known as *Acteosaurus,* was a semi-aquatic creature that lived in Europe during the Cretaceous period. Another group of lizards, the mosasaurs, took up a fully aquatic marine lifestyle and were spectacularly successful, reaching lengths of over twenty feet before dying out in the same mass extinction that killed the dinosaurs. There is some evidence that modern snakes are descended from a member of the same group of reptiles as the mosasaurs.

Biology and Anatomy

Although they are closely related to the snakes, lizards somewhat resemble the amphibian salamanders, with which they are often confused. Lizards can be distinguished from salamanders by their dry, scaly skin, their visible external ears, their moveable eyelids, the claws on the tips of their toes and their preference for generally drier and hotter habitats.

Ranging in size from two inches to over ten feet, lizards, like all herps, are ectotherms. Because they cannot produce their own body heat, they are dependent upon outside sources and must alter their behavior in order to thermoregulate—moving from sun to shade and back to keep a constant body temperature. The popular term "cold-blooded" is not very accurate, as many lizards maintain body temperatures of over 100 degrees. By basking in sunlight, lizards can maintain high body temperatures even if the air temperature is somewhat cool, because lizard skin absorbs heat much better than the surrounding air. Lizards prefer higher temperatures than other herps.

Because they don't need energy to produce body heat, ectotherms do not need to eat as much food as do similarly sized mammals. The reduced need for food, combined with their ability to conserve water, has made lizards one of the most successful colonizers of hot, arid desert regions.

Eyes

Lizards have excellent vision and can detect shapes and movement at astonishingly long distances. They have excellent color vision, and they use a great deal of visual signalling in their mating and territorial displays. Many lizards have bright patches of blue, red or yellow, which they display to potential mates or rivals. Nearly all lizards have moveable eyelids, and most also have a clear nictating membrane that sweeps the eyeball and keeps it moist. The geckos lack eyelids and keep their eyes clean by licking them with their long tongues.

Skin

The skin of a lizard is dry, scaly and waterproof to protect the body against moisture loss. The scales are formed from folds in the outer layer, called the epidermis. This outer layer is dead and made of the protein keratin. Because the epidermis is not flexible and cannot grow, the lizard must periodically shed its skin and grow a new epidermis. When the old skin becomes too tight, a

new one will form underneath. To remove the old layer, the lizard uses fluids to swell its body, causing the epidermis to crack and peel off in large flakes, that are usually then consumed by the lizard.

Tongue

Unlike snakes, lizards have a well-developed sense of taste in their tongues. The tongue of most lizards is thick and fleshy and cannot be extended far from the mouth. Only a few lizards, including the monitors, possess the deeply forked tongue typical of snakes. Most lizards, however, have a Jacobson's organ in their mouths similar to that of snakes, which senses chemical traces in the environment. Lizards can often be observed taste-testing their surroundings by touching their tongues to the ground. Only the chameleons use

their tongues to capture food; other lizards just run up to prey and grab it in their jaws.

Hemipenes

Like snakes, lizards have two paired sexual organs in the base of the tail known as "hemipenes." During mating, only one of the hemipenes is used. Male lizards are also distinguished by the presence of large pre-anal and femoral pores, which are found running along the insides of the thighs. These pores are small and nonfunctional in female lizards. In males, they secrete a waxy substance which helps the male grip the female during mating. The wax is rubbed onto the female's body, stimulating her to lift her tail so the male can insert one of his hemipenes. All lizards practice internal fertilization.

Stomach

The feeding habits of lizards can be divided into three types. The vast majority of lizards are insectivorous and eat bugs, spiders and other small arthropods. A few families such as the monitors are predators and eat rodents, birds, snakes and other lizards. The larger monitors can even catch and kill goats or pigs. Only a small number of modern lizards are herbivorous plant eaters. These include the green iguana, the chuckwalla and the mastigures. The herbivorous lizards have symbiotic bacteria living in

The dry, scaly skin of lizards can be seen on this Bearded Dragon.

their digestive tract which break down plant cellulose into sugars which the lizard can digest.

Heart

Like most herps, lizards have three-chambered hearts in which oxygenated blood from the lungs is allowed to mix with depleted blood from the rest of the body. Although lizards tend to have higher internal body temperatures than most reptiles and are thus more active, they do not have great stamina and tire easily. The monitors are unique among lizards in having the ventricle of their heart divided by a narrow channel, which greatly reduces the mixing of blood and enables them to use oxygen more efficiently than other lizards and to remain active for longer time spans.

Teeth

Lizards do not have socketed teeth; the teeth are either set into the inner surface of the jawbone (pleurodont teeth) or are attached to the top surface of the jawbones (acrodont teeth). A lizard's teeth continuously fall out during its life and are quickly replaced. Although the agamid lizards sometimes show a differentiation in tooth structure, in most lizards the teeth are cone-like and are all the same size and shape. These teeth are used to hold the prey before it is swallowed whole, and most lizards thus cannot chew their food. In the

monitor lizards, the teeth have serrated edges for cutting pieces of flesh, enabling them to slice pieces from their prey and thus eat animals much larger than they could swallow whole.

The venomous gila monsters have simple grooves in a few of their teeth which allow venom to enter the wound when the lizard bites its prey.

Tail

Nearly all lizards can voluntarily detach their tails when threatened by a predator. Muscle spasms will cause the detached tail to thrash around, distracting the predator while the lizard makes its escape. The tail detaches along a pre-formed fracture plane in the middle of the tail vertebrae. A new tail will grow to replace the detached

one, although the new tail will not be as long or as brightly colored as the old one. If the tail is mechanically severed between the vertebrae rather than along the fracture planes, however, it will not grow back.

Toes

Most lizards have five toes on each foot with a claw on the end of each toe. In some species, however, the number of toes may vary from four to five on the same individual. The most unusual lizard toes belong to the geckos. Some species of gecko have claws that can be retracted like those of cats. All geckos have toes that are crossed with numerous ridges, carrying thousands of tiny hooks. These hooks grasp at the minute irregularities which are present even in the smoothest surfaces, enabling geckos to walk

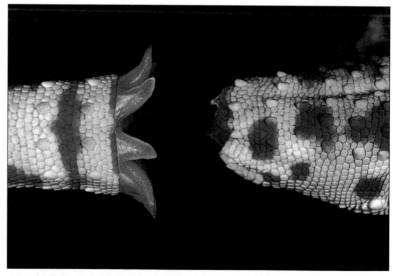

A lizard will detach its tail along a pre-formed fracture plane (tokay gecko).

up glass panes and even across ceilings.

Pelvic Girdle

Like all reptiles, lizards' limbs project to the sides of the pelvic girdle. The body is thus supported on the bent legs, and the lizard looks like it is in the middle of a push-up. Even though some desert lizards can hit speeds of fifteen miles per hour, they cannot maintain this speed for long. Several species of lizard can run on their two hind legs for short distances to escape predators, although no lizard is habitually bipedal. About half of all lizard families have members with either no legs or legs so small that they cannot be used for walking. Even legless lizards, however, have well-developed pelvic girdles.

Ears

Most lizards have large external ear openings on the sides of the head, which often appear as clear windows or patches. In some burrowing species, the ears may be very small and perhaps completely covered with scales. Most lizards, however, have excellent hearing. Lizards apparently cannot hear as wide a range of frequencies as humans do, but they are much more acute in those frequencies that they do hear. Despite their excellent sense of hearing, most lizards are mute. The geckos are the only lizards capable of vocalization.

A lizard's ears resemble patches on the side of its head (green iguana).

Pineal Gland

Most lizards have a large pineal gland, often referred to as the "third eye," at the top of their heads between their eyes. This appears as a clear window or patch. Although it is known that the pineal body functions as a light sensor and can distinguish between light and dark, its exact purpose is unclear. The most widely accepted theory is that it serves as a "light meter" to measure the intensity of sunlight so that the lizard can thermoregulate more effectively. The pineal gland may also measure the length of the day, thereby providing cues for hibernation, mating seasons and so on.

Diseases

Lizards are subject to many of the same diseases as turtles and snakes, including mouth rot, worms and respiratory infections. However, lizards also have a number of health problems that are not found as often among turtles or snakes.

Metabolic Bone Disease

Lizards (particularly iguanids) occasionally suffer from a calcium deficiency because they are commonly fed an exclusive diet of crickets, which do not contain much usable calcium. Calcium deficiency results in weak and brittle bones and may produce lumps or deformities in the legs or jaws. To prevent calcium problems, crickets should be dusted with a vitamin and mineral supplement before they are fed to lizards. Also, lizards should be fed a wide variety of prey insects, rather than just crickets.

A particular form of calcium deficiency, common to iguanas but also sometimes found in other lizards, is Metabolic Bone Disease, or MBD. MBD can be caused by too little calcium in the diet or by a lack of sufficient ultraviolet wavelengths. Lizards use the ultraviolet wavelengths in natural sunlight to manufacture vitamin D3 in their skin. This vitamin enables the lizard to extract calcium from its food for use in building bones. If there is insufficient calcium in the food or if the lizard is deprived of UV light, its body will react by extracting calcium from its own bones, causing them to become soft and fibrous. The limbs appear swollen and fat as the bones begin to break down. The jawbones will also appear lumpy and swollen. Death is certain without treatment.

MBD is treated by providing adequate amounts of UV light and by adding calcium supplements to the diet. To help prevent MBD, the lizard's food can be sprinkled with a pinch of phosphorus-free calcium supplement every other meal.

Hypercalcemia

In contrast to MBD, which occurs when there is too little calcium in the diet, hypercalcemia is the result of too much calcium in the diet. It is usually caused by mistakenly placing too much vitamin supplement in the food. Another common cause is feeding animal proteins to herbivorous lizards such as iguanas.

The excess calcium causes bone damage, kidney failure and changes in the heartbeat. Because none of these symptoms may be apparent to the keeper, they may go unnoticed until it is too late. A lizard with hypercalcemia requires a vet right away.

Nail Trimming

Large lizards such as iguanas, tegus or monitors, have razor-sharp claws which can cause injury to their keeper if not properly maintained. These nails should be periodically clipped or trimmed.

The lizard should be restrained with one hand while the other hand does the trimming. If necessary, an excitable or aggressive lizard can be wrapped in a towel to prevent it from struggling or tail-lashing.

The best instrument for trimming a reptile's nails are the clippers used to trim the nails of dogs. These resemble a short-nosed pair of scissors with a half-moon shaped cutting area. The semicircular shape prevents the claw from moving when pressure is applied and allows the cut to be made very precisely.

In most lizards, the base of the claw is clear and the sharp tip is black. Only the very end of the sharp tip should be clipped off. If the claw is trimmed near the base, it will bleed and cause pain to the reptile (and will very likely cause it to resent any future nail-trimming). If you accidentally trim a nail too close to the base, a dab of cornstarch will stop the bleeding.

Egg Binding

Egg binding is an affliction that can affect any female reptile (even live-bearers) but usually strikes lizards such as iguanas. In gravid females, the eggs are unable to pass through the cloacal opening and are retained in the oviduct where they can cause fatal internal injuries. The causes are varied—improper diet may play a role, and lizards that are denied a proper substrate for egg-laying may retain them too long and become egg-bound. Even female lizards who have not been mated will sometimes develop a clutch of infertile eggs, which can become bound just like fertile eggs.

Egg-bound lizards will have swollen hindquarters, caused by the retained eggs pressing against the body wall. They will be lethargic and inactive. As they weaken, the female lizards make frantic efforts to dig a nest and deposit eggs. The cloacal wall may sometimes be prolapsed from the pressure and protrude outside the body. Any lizard that does not lay a full clutch of eggs within forty-eight hours and still has noticeable eggs in the body, should be treated for egg binding.

HELP HERPS

You can help to save the habitat of endangered herps. One way is to contribute to the Center for Ecosystem Survival (CES). This organization raises money to purchase critical areas of habitat around the world and sets them aside as wildlife refuges. According to the size of the contribution, the donor is given an honorary deed for a parcel of land. CES has helped to protect over 11 million acres of tropical habitat.

Egg binding is a serious disorder and can be fatal in a matter of days. Sometimes the lizard can be induced to pass the retained eggs by an injection of hormones. In instances where the retention is the result of egg abnormality or a blockage in the reproductive tract, the eggs can sometimes be aspirated—their contents are sucked out by a hollow needle, which makes the egg smaller and sometimes enables the female to pass it normally. If neither of these methods work, however, surgery will be necessary to open up the abdominal cavity and remove the bound eggs.

The ameiva is an agitated lizard that is difficult to handle.

Species Descriptions

Ameiva
(Ameiva ameiva)

Level: Intermediate
Size: Medium
Habitat: Savannah, Terrestrial

Biology
The ameiva is a member of the teiid family and is closely related to the tegu and the American whiptail lizards. It is native to Central and Latin America, where it known as the "jungle runner," but it has been introduced into several other tropical areas, including Florida. It is a nervous, aggressive lizard that never really becomes tame and is difficult to handle.

Housing
In the wild, ameivas inhabit open sunny grasslands with dry sandy soil. In captivity, they require large cages with a number of hide boxes to feel secure. Because they are large and active, they will quickly dismantle any cage furnishings and are best kept in a bare tank with a gravel substrate. A water dish is necessary, and a hot spot for basking must be provided, as well as a source of unfiltered ultraviolet light.

Feeding
Ameivas are active predators and will hunt down and eat birds and their eggs, small mammals and other reptiles. Smaller specimens eat insects and earthworms. Captives can be fed a staple of rodents, supplemented with canned dog food which has been fortified with vitamin and calcium supplement powder.

Breeding
Ameivas are not often bred in captivity. In the wild, they lay two to four eggs per clutch, buried in a warm damp spot. Females may lay several clutches throughout the year after a single mating.

Asian Water Dragon
(Physignathus turcicus)

Level: Novice
Size: Medium
Habitat: Tropical, Semi-Arboreal/Semi-Aquatic

Biology
The Asian water dragon, also known as the Thai water dragon, is native

to the rain forests of Southeast Asia. It is very similar to the green iguana in appearance and habitat, being a large green lizard with a black-banded tail. At an adult size of about two feet, it is largely arboreal and spends much of its time in trees. A crest of spinelike scales runs down the lizard's back. Unlike the iguana, however, the water dragon is a member of the agamid family of lizards. They are nervous lizards that are prone to panic and never really settle down.

Housing

As its name indicates, the water dragon is an excellent swimmer and spends much time in the water. The cage must be provided with a water pan large enough for the lizard to swim and bathe. Water dragons also require a number of branches for climbing and hide boxes where they can retreat to feel secure. The cage must be large and roomy as these lizards are large and active.

Warm humid conditions are necessary with daytime temperatures in the 80s, dropping to the 70s at night. Water dragons also need access to unfiltered ultraviolet light.

Feeding

Unlike the green iguanas, which are almost totally herbivorous, water dragons are largely carnivorous and eat insects and small vertebrates. Captives can be fed crickets or pinkie mice. They will also occasionally accept pieces of ripe fruit and green leafy vegetables.

Breeding

Mating takes place during the tropical rainy season. Female water dragons lay up to five clutches of eggs per year with ten to fifteen eggs per clutch, making this one of the most prolific of lizards. The hatchlings measure about four inches long and are miniature replicas of their parents. They should be removed to a separate cage and provided with

plenty of food and sources of ultraviolet light. Hatchling water dragons reach maturity in about three years.

Basilisk
(Basiliscus species)

Level: Intermediate
Size: Medium
Habitat: Tropical, Semi-Aquatic, Semi-Arboreal

Biology

There are several species of basilisk lizard, all of them native to the rain forests of Central America. The most common in the pet trade is the brown basilisk (*Basilicus vetata*) and the much larger green or plumed basilisk (*Basilicus plumifrons*). A green basilisk can reach a length of almost three feet.

The basilisk is best known for its ability to run on two legs to escape a predator, like a small bipedal dinosaur. The long tail is used as a balancing rod while the lizard is running. If a third or more of the tail is broken off, the basilisk can no longer run.

An even more surprising habit is the basilisk's ability to run across the surface of water without sinking, a talent which has earned it the nickname "Jesus Christ lizard." This feat is made possible by the large spreading toes, which distribute the weight and trap large air bubbles to keep the lizard from sinking.

The green water dragon closely resembles the green iguana.

Basilisks have the unusual ability to run for short distances on their hind legs—they have even been known to run on water. (green basilisk).

and these hatch in about ten weeks. The hatchlings are about five inches long and are miniature replicas of their parents. Young males do not develop their dorsal crests until they reach sexual maturity at about the age of one and one-half to two years.

Bearded Dragon (Pogona vitticeps)

Level: Novice
Size: Medium
Habitat: Savannah, Semi-Arboreal

Biology

Bearded dragons are native to hot dry areas of Australia. The name refers to the large number of spines that line the skin of the throat. These normally lie flat, but when the lizard feels threatened, it inflates its throat, causing the spines to stick out in an intimidating display.

Bearded dragons can reach lengths of up to two feet.

Housing

The basilisk is native to the rain forests of Central America and requires warm and humid conditions. Daytime temperatures should be in the 80s, dropping to the 70s at night. A large cage is required with lots of vertical space, tree branches for climbing and a large water pan for soaking.

Like most lizards, basilisks cannot store Vitamin D in their bodies and need access to unfiltered ultraviolet light to manufacture this nutrient.

Feeding

Basilisks are almost entirely insectivorous and feed on bugs and other arthropods, which they find in tree branches or along the water's edge. Captives can be fed crickets which have been dusted with vitamin and mineral supplements. Large specimens may take pinkie mice. Individual lizards may occasionally eat plant materials.

Breeding

Male basilisks can be distinguished by their large, showy dorsal crests, which the females lack. Five to twelve eggs are laid in sandy soil,

Standard coloring for a bearded dragon is a light brown, but they are also available in more striking color phases, such as red.

These lizards have recently become very popular in the pet trade and are now widely captive-bred. They are available in a number of color phases or "morphs." The normal coloring is tan or light brown. Other phases include red, yellow and gold.

Housing

Bearded dragons are large and active and require large cages with extensive room. A single adult will require at least a forty-gallon cage. The temperature in the cage should be around 80 degrees with a basking spot that reaches between 100 and 110 degrees. A strong source of ultraviolet light is necessary.

Feeding

Although bearded dragons are largely insectivorous, they also eat an amount of plant material. The best

Bearded dragons enjoy a good cricket.

staple food is crickets, supplemented occasionally with other insects. Leafy green vegetables and fruits can be offered every other day.

In the wild, bearded dragons live in areas where food is scarce at some times of the year, so they are capable of storing large amounts of energy in fat bodies in their abdomens. In captivity, however, they should be fed year-round.

Although bearded dragons will sometimes drink from a shallow dish, they prefer to lick droplets of water and should be misted every day.

Breeding

Bearded dragons are widely captive-bred. Males can be recognized by their larger heads, large femoral pores underneath their legs and their increased willingness to perform their "push-up" territorial display.

A clutch may contain as many as twenty-five eggs. The young grow rapidly, reaching a length of six inches in just eight weeks and attaining adult size in around one year. Bearded dragons are capable of breeding at one or one and one-half years old.

Blue Bellied Lizard (Sceleporus occidentalis)

Level: Novice
Size: Small
Habitat: Savannah, Terrestrial/Burrower

Biology

The blue bellied lizard, also known as the western fence lizard, is a common inhabitant of the American west. It is a member of the *Sceloporus* genus and is closely related to the spiny lizards. It is an inhabitant of dry arid canyon regions where it darts among the rocks in search of insect prey. Blue bellies are excellent climbers and can often ascend even vertical rock faces.

To avoid predators, they are capable of altering their skin color, becoming darker or lighter to match their surroundings. They often spend the night buried in sand or loose gravel. Blue bellied lizards can reach lengths of up to eight inches.

Housing

In the wild, blue bellied lizards prefer dry rocky areas with plenty of hiding places. They are not large lizards, but they are very active and require a large cage. The males are territorial and pugnacious, often engaging in ritualistic head-bobbing and push-ups to warn away potential rivals. They are best kept in a group of one male and two or three females.

They need hot dry conditions with a hot spot for basking and a source of ultraviolet light. A large rock pile will provide hiding spots, and a tree branch will provide places to climb. A sand substrate is best for these lizards. Although blue bellied lizards are active and fast, they rarely move more than a few hundred feet from their home area.

Feeding

Blue bellied lizards are entirely insectivorous. They will catch and eat any small arthropods, including insects, spiders and other invertebrates. Captives can be fed a diet of crickets that have been dusted with a vitamin supplement.

Breeding

Male blue bellied lizards can be easily recognized by their bright blue throat and flank patches. These serve as recognition signals, and if they are painted over, the male will be treated as a female by other lizards. Breeding takes place in the spring, and from five to fifteen eggs are laid in the sand from May to July. Older females tend to lay larger clutches than younger lizards. The eggs hatch in about two months. Hatchling blue bellied lizards are about two inches long and reach maturity within two years.

Cuban Anole
(Anolis equestris)

Level: Novice
Size: Medium
Habitat: Tropical, Arboreal

Biology

The Cuban anole, as the name indicates, is native to Cuba and the Caribbean. It is also known as the Knight anole. In appearance and habits, Cuban anoles are very similar to the common green anole, but they are much larger, reaching lengths of up to eighteen inches, the largest of the 150 or so members of the *Anolis* genus to be found throughout Latin America.

Cuban anoles are exclusively arboreal and rarely descend to the ground. Their major predators are snakes, and Cuban anoles often give a defensive reaction—puffing up the body and extending the dewlap—to anything that looks remotely snakelike, such as a hose or rope. In captivity, they are capable of giving a painful bite, but they tame quickly and are not usually aggressive.

Cuban anoles were introduced to Florida in 1952 and have now established themselves there.

Housing

Cuban anoles require housing similar to that for green anoles but correspondingly larger. The cage should have lots of vertical space with plenty of tree branches and plants for climbing. A strong source of ultraviolet light is necessary, as is a hot spot for basking. Moderately high humidity and temperatures in the 80s are required.

Cuban anoles will not drink from a water dish, and their cage must be misted every morning so they can lick the droplets off the

Cuban anoles rarely descend to the ground.

leaves. Males are territorial and should not be kept together.

Feeding

Cuban anoles are insectivorous and will eat such large insects as locusts, grasshoppers and beetles. They will also sometimes accept pinkie mice or other small vertebrates.

Breeding

Male Cuban anoles can be recognized by their large pink dewlaps, which they will often extend as part of a territorial head-bobbing display. Cuban anoles are not often bred in captivity, and most of the individuals in the pet trade have been wild-caught. In the wild, breeding takes place in the summer. The eggs are laid in damp soil and hatch several weeks later.

Curly Tail Lizard
(Leiocephalus carinatus)

Level: Novice
Size: Small
Habitat: Savannah, Terrestrial

Biology

Curly tail lizards, also known as Lion lizards, are native to Haiti and the other islands of the Caribbean. They grow to a length of ten inches. The common name comes from the male's habit of carrying his tail arched high over the back as a territorial display. Curly tails are fast and active, and although they are relatively easy to care for, they cannot be handled. They have been introduced to southern Florida and have established themselves there.

Housing

The natural habitat of the curly tail lizard is dry scrub brush. In captivity, they need a semi-arid terrarium with a sand substrate and lots of rocks to provide hiding places. They bask often and need temperatures in the 80s with a hot spot and source of ultraviolet light for basking. They are nervous and very fast, requiring large cages. Curly tails do best in small groups of one male and two or three females. The males are strongly territorial and should not be housed together.

Feeding

Curly tails are typical insectivores, running down and capturing insects and other arthropods. Captives do well on a diet of crickets, dusted with vitamin and mineral supplements.

Breeding

Male curly tails curve their tail over the back as a territorial display instead of the head-bobbing and push-ups which are more typical of desert lizards. They are not often bred in captivity. In the wild, breeding takes place in spring, and the eggs are laid in summer, shallowly buried in warm patches of sand. They hatch several months later.

Day Gecko
(Phelsuma species)

Level: Intermediate
Size: Small to Medium
Habitat: Tropical, Semi-Arboreal

Biology

Day geckos are spectacularly colored with an electric blue, red and green pattern. As the name suggests, and unlike most geckos, they are diurnal and active during the daytime. There are several species of day gecko, all native to Mauritius, Madagascar and other islands of the Indian Ocean. They range in size from small lizards of less than five inches to the giant day gecko from Madagascar, which can measure up to one foot in length.

Day geckos are legally protected in most of their native habitats, and nearly all individuals available in the United States have been captive-bred.

Curly tails are fast, active lizards that will not tolerate handling.

A giant day gecko can grow to be one foot long.

Housing

Day geckos are fiercely territorial. Males will not tolerate any rivals in their tank, and even established groups or pairs will not tolerate new-comers of either sex. The males and females will even squabble with each other outside of the breeding season.

Day geckos require large tanks with lots of plants and vegetation. Several pieces of hollow bamboo stem should be added to serve as retreats and hiding places. Like all diurnal lizards, they require a source of unfiltered ultraviolet light and a hot spot for basking.

No water dish is necessary, as day geckos will not drink standing water. Instead, the cage must be misted daily to allow them to drink and to keep the humidity at acceptably high levels.

Feeding

Like all geckos, day geckos are largely insectivorous and can be fed crickets, flies and other insects. For proper nutrition, these should be dusted with vitamin and calcium powders. Day geckos also like sweet food and will often lick sugar cubes or drops of honey that are placed in their tank.

Breeding

It is extremely difficult to distinguish male day geckos from females. The females tend to be slightly smaller and have slightly less brilliant colors. They also lack pre-anal pores on their undersides. Breeding pairs must both be of approximately the same size, or the smaller individual will be continually attacked and harassed.

Breeding takes place in the spring and summer after an elaborate ritual involving lots of head-bobbing and tail-waving. The eggs are usually laid in pairs, attached to the inside of a hollow bamboo tube or other sheltered spot. Up to six clutches may be laid in the course of a summer. The eggs should be removed and artificially incubated.

The eggs hatch in about ten weeks and are temperature-dependent for sex. Accordingly, the hatchlings, about one inch long, are usually of the same sex. They reach sexual maturity in about one year.

The gold dust day gecko illustrates the remarkable coloring of this species.

Glass Lizard
(Ophisaurus species)

Level: Intermediate
Size: Large
Habitat: Tropical, Burrower

Biology

The long, legless glass lizard is often mistaken for a snake and is often referred to as the "glass snake." It is actually a member of the anguid family of lizards and closely related to the alligator lizards. The glass lizard can be distinguished from snakes by its moveable eyelids and its visible ear holes at the side of the head.

The common name of this lizard refers to its ability to defend itself by casting off its tail, which is much longer than the rest of its body and often breaks into several pieces. According to folklore, the glass lizard breaks into pieces if it is struck, but later the pieces will reassemble themselves. This, of course, never actually happens. The glass lizard can regenerate a lost tail, but it will be a different color than the original.

They are nervous and defensive lizards, and specimens that still have their original tails are rare. Glass lizards have lived up to twenty-five years in captivity.

Housing

At an average length of twenty-six inches and a record length of over

Inasmuch as they have no legs, it is not surprising that glass lizards are often taken for snakes.

three feet, glass lizards are the longest lizards in North America and therefore require sizable cages. Their natural habitats are the meadows and grassy areas of the eastern United States. Glass lizards can be kept on a gravel or soil substrate with lots of rocks and branches for climbing and hiding, but they are excellent burrowers and will usually stay out of sight beneath the substrate. They prefer temperatures in the high 70s or low 80s, and although they are diurnal, they do not often bask and do not need a hot spot.

Glass lizards are nervous and defensive at first, and although they do not usually attempt to bite, they may cast off their tail and expel fluid from their anal sacks. They quickly settle down, however,

and become tame enough to handle.

Feeding

Glass lizards feed on a wide variety of prey items, including insects, spiders, snails, slugs, bird eggs and smaller reptiles. Captives can be fed crickets, other insects and sometimes baby mice. They can also be trained to eat small pieces of raw beef or liver or a mixture of chopped meat and raw egg. Vitamin and calcium supplements should be added to all of their food.

Breeding

Glass lizards are not easy to breed in captivity. Mating takes place in May, and six to ten eggs are laid in early June in a shallow nest scooped into the soil. Glass lizards

Like most geckos, the Mediterranean gecko has pads on its toes that allow it to climb up walls and even to run across ceilings upside down. It is the only lizard found in North America that has a voice—it produces a characteristic faint mouselike squeak. Mediterranean geckos are widely available in the pet trade.

Housing

Although Mediterranean geckos are native to dry rocky areas, they are remarkably adaptive and have adjusted to living in hot humid areas like Florida, as well as cooler areas of Asia. In captivity, they can be kept in a typical semi-arid terrarium with several rock piles to provide hiding places. These geckos are shy and insecure, spending the entire day hiding in crevices under rocks and emerging at night to hunt for insect prey.

Because they are nocturnal, Mediterranean geckos do not require a basking spot or access to ultraviolet light, but the temperature in their cage should not be allowed to drop below 75 degrees.

Feeding

Like all geckos, the Mediterranean gecko is insectivorous and actively hunts down flies, mosquitoes, beetles and other insects. Captives can be fed small crickets and other bugs. Mealworms should be avoided, as their hard exoskeletons are indigestible and can cause blockages.

Breeding

The Mediterranean gecko breeds readily under a wide variety of environmental conditions, which has been a large factor in its ability to become widely established in non-native areas. If kept in a small group of four or five lizards, they will breed almost continuously. Mating takes place in the spring with clutches of eggs laid throughout the summer. The eggs are sticky when laid and often fastened to a tree branch or to the side of the terrarium. Each clutch contains two eggs, which invariably produce two individuals of the same sex. Mediterranean geckos are believed to exhibit temperature-dependent sex determination. Unlike most lizard eggs, which are leathery and flexible, the eggs of Mediterranean geckos are hard and brittle like bird eggs. The eggs hatch in about three months. The hatchlings should be moved to a separate tank where they will reach sexual maturity within a year.

Nile Monitor
(Varanus niloticus)

Level: Advanced
Size: Extra Large
Habitat: Tropical, Semi-Aquatic

Biology

Nile monitors are large, aggressive lizards that can be difficult and even dangerous to handle. They are not for the beginning herper. As juveniles, they have a bright,

A juvenile Nile monitor has a bright black and yellow pattern.

attractive black and yellow pattern, but this coloration fades with age. Adults are usually plain brown or tan. A full-grown Nile monitor can measure up to six feet long, but they are not very heavy-bodied lizards and do not weigh as much as some other monitors of the same size. As the name suggests, they are native to the Nile River Valley in Egypt. Nile monitors are reported to be more intelligent than most lizards.

Housing

Nile monitors require extensive accommodations if they are to be kept in good health. They require temperatures in the 80s with a basking spot of at least 90 degrees. They also need a powerful source of unfiltered ultraviolet light.

Although they spend much of their time on land, they have laterally compressed tails like an alligator, making them excellent swimmers, and a water pool large enough for them to soak in must be provided.

Feeding

Nile monitors are powerful and active predators with strong teeth and heavy claws on their front feet for disemboweling prey animals. Although they are capable of bringing down animals as large as sheep, Nile monitors in the wild prefer such fare as birds and small mammals. They are a major predator of turtle and crocodile eggs and hatchlings, and in turn, adult crocodiles are a major predator of Nile monitors.

In captivity, young Nile monitors can be fed a diet of whole rodents, supplemented with canned dog food to which vitamin and calcium powder has been added. Larger specimens must be fed whole prey such as rabbits, chickens and raw eggs. A commercial lizard food composed largely of horse meat is available and can be used as a supplement to whole prey animals. Adult Nile monitors are voracious eaters and are very expensive to feed.

Breeding

Because of their large size and specialized breeding habits, Nile monitors are not often bred in captivity. In the wild, male monitors may rear up on their hind legs and wrestle with each other to establish mating rights. The eggs are typically laid inside termite nests after the spring rains have softened them enough for the lizard to dig through with its heavy claws. The eggs measure over four inches in length and hatch in a few months.

Plated Lizard
(Gerrhosaurus species)

Level: Intermediate
Size: Medium
Habitat: Savannah, Terrestrial

Biology

There are several species of plated lizards available in the pet trade. All of them are native to dry, hot

The plated lizard gets its name from the tile-like scales that cover its body.

areas of Africa. They can be recognized by their long pointed heads and the longitudinal groove running down both sides of their bodies. The name "plated lizard" refers to the large rectangular scales which cover the body like tiles.

Plated lizards can reach lengths of up to two feet long. They are nervous and defensive, never really becoming tame, but they do not often try to bite—their primary defensive tactic is to lash out with their long spiny tail.

Housing

Plated lizards are native to dry grasslands and scrub areas, and they do well in large cages (at least seven or eight square feet) with a sand substrate and a lot of rocks for hiding and basking. They require temperatures in the 80s and a hot spot for basking, as well as a source of unfiltered ultraviolet light. They are nervous and shy, often refusing to eat unless they have a retreat or hide box where they can feel secure.

Feeding

Young plated lizards are almost entirely insectivorous and will eat crickets, waxworms and earthworms. Larger adults will also eat small rodents or other vertebrates. They become more herbivorous as they get older, and adults will accept fresh fruits such as apples, strawberries and cantaloupes. They get most of their moisture from the fruits they eat, but their cage should be misted daily to allow them to lick up the droplets.

Breeding

Although plated lizards are not particularly difficult to keep in captivity, captive breeding has only rarely been accomplished, and most of the individuals available in the United States have been wild caught. The eggs are laid in shallow sand nests and hatch in about three months. In some species, the nests are guarded by the female; in others, they are left on their own.

Savannah Monitor
(Varanus exanthematicus)

Level: Intermediate
Size: Large
Habitat: Savannah, Terrestrial

Biology

The Savannah monitor has recently become very popular in the pet trade and is widely available. Unfortunately, many people buy juvenile Savannah monitors without any real idea of what they are getting into. Although the Savannah monitor is one of the least aggressive and smallest of the monitors and often becomes quite tame, it can still reach lengths of up to four feet and is a powerful animal that must be handled carefully. Savannah monitors are native to the dry grasslands of Africa.

Housing

Although the Savannah monitor does not grow as large as some of the other varanid lizards, it is still a big, active animal and requires extensive accommodations. Smaller individuals can be kept in sturdy wooden cages with plenty of room for wandering. Because they will quickly destroy any cage furnishings, their accommodations should be sparse with a plain gravel substrate, a hide box, a water dish and a few large rocks.

Although a relatively gentle monitor lizard, the Savannah monitor is nonetheless a large, strong animal.

Adults can be given the free run of a room, so long as they are kept warm and provided with a hot spot for basking. Like all diurnal lizards, Savannah monitors need access to unfiltered ultraviolet light.

Feeding

Savannah monitors, like all monitors, are active predators and will eat any smaller animal that they can overpower. In captivity, they should be fed whole prey animals such as rodents or birds. Pre-killed or frozen prey is preferable to live food animals. They will also sometimes eat whole raw chicken eggs.

This diet can be supplemented with a commercial monitor food made from horse meat, which should be fortified with vitamin and calcium supplements. Large Savannah monitors will easily eat one or two rodents a day.

Breeding

Because of the space requirements and the voracious appetites of the young lizards, Savannah monitors are not often bred in captivity except by professional reptile breeders and wholesalers. The large, oval eggs are laid in shallow nests in sand or soil. The hatchlings are around ten inches long and can grow quickly if well fed.

Skink
(Eumeces species)

Level: Novice to Intermediate
Size: Small to Large
Habitat: Varies by species

Biology

The skinks are one of the largest family of lizards with over 600 species distributed on nearly every continent. Seventeen skink species are native to North America. They are all very similar in appearance and habits and can be cared for in much the same way.

A typical skink is about twelve inches long, although some species, such as the blue tongue skink and the monkey tailed skink, can grow to two and one-half feet long. Most skinks have smooth shiny scales which are suited for burrowing, and their skin feels stiff because it is reinforced by small bony plates called osteoderms.

Housing

With the exception of the desert-dwelling sandfish, which require hot, dry, desert terrariums with a deep sand substrate, most skinks will do well in a typical woodland terrarium with a deep substrate of soil or moss. Temperature requirements will vary according to the natural habitat of each species, but in general the range of 75 to 85 degrees is suitable with a moderately high humidity.

Skinks do not bask and seem to be able to thrive without access to ultraviolet light. Some of the larger skinks are cannibalistic and cannot be kept with smaller reptiles.

Both the monkey tailed skink (left) and the blue tongue skink (right) can grow up to two and one-half feet in length.

Unlike other skinks, sandfish need a hot, dry, desert environment.

Feeding

All skinks are carnivorous and spend most of their time rooting through the leaf litter searching for insects, earthworms, slugs and snails. The larger species will also eat small vertebrates such as rodents, snakes and smaller lizards.

Breeding

The breeding habits of the skinks vary from species to species. Most species lay eggs, with mating taking place in the spring and clutches of up to a dozen eggs laid in early summer in leaf litter or damp soil. Many of the *Eumeces* species of skink, such as the five lined skink, will brood the eggs and guard them until they hatch. In a level of parental care that is unusual among lizards, these females will even gather up lost eggs and can find them by smell if they are moved. Many skinks from cooler areas do not lay eggs but produce live young. In some of these species, the female produces a primitive placenta like that found in mammals to nourish the developing young.

Tegu
(Tupinambis teguixin)

Level: Advanced
Size: Large
Habitat: Tropical, Terrestrial

Biology

Tegus are large, aggressive lizards from Latin America that can grow up to four feet long. They are members of the teiid family and are closely related to the North American whiptail lizards.

There are two geographic races to this species, known as the black and white tegu and the golden tegu. The black and white tegu is boldly patterned with white bands on a glossy black background, while the golden tegu is a shiny tan color. The black and white race is reputed to have a better temperament, but both are nervous and defensive and can be dangerous to handle. They are not suitable for the beginning herper.

Housing

Tegus are tropical animals and require warm, humid conditions. Daytime temperatures should be in the 80s, dropping to the 70s at night. Tegus are also large and active and require an extensive well-built enclosure with a large water pool and several basking sites.

Feeding

Tegus are large, active predators and will eat any animal that they can overpower. Captives can be fed whole, pre-killed or frozen rodents. Large individuals will eat chickens or rabbits. They will also occasionally accept raw eggs. Some tegus can be taught to accept pieces of raw beef or liver, and canned dog food can also be used as a supplement to whole prey. These foods should be fortified with a vitamin and mineral powder.

Tegus are aggressive and do not make good pets for the novice (black and white tegu).

A few tegus will accept occasional pieces of fruit in their diet.

Breeding

Because of the space requirements that a breeding pair of tegus would need, they are not often bred in captivity except in some zoos. In the wild, female tegus use their powerful claws to rip open termite nests and lay their eggs there. Once the termites have resealed the breach, the eggs have a safe, warm and humid area in which to complete their development. The newly emerged hatchlings then dig their way out of their enclosure.

The tokay gecko's sticky toe pads allow it to climb up glass and even to run across ceilings.

Tokay Gecko (Gekko gecko)

Level: Novice
Size: Medium
Habitat: Tropical, Arboreal

Biology

Tokay geckos are large, brightly colored lizards than can grow up to one foot in length. Although they are attractively colored with patches of orange or red on a sky blue background, they are nervous and aggressive, biting viciously when handled. They are native to the rain forests of Southeast Asia but have been widely introduced throughout the world. The name "tokay" comes from the characteristic clicking call made by the males.

Housing

Like all geckos, tokays are climbers and have pads on their toes that allow them to climb up glass and even run upside down across ceilings. They require large, well-built cages if escapes are to be prevented. A large number of vertical tree branches or pieces of wood must be provided for climbing, and a hide box or crevice is needed to serve as a retreat.

Tokay geckos are nocturnal and do not need a basking light or ultraviolet lighting, although they do require warm, humid conditions. They are territorial, and each lizard will establish a home base in a crevice or hole. It will not wander far from this area and will defend its territory against any intruders.

Feeding

Tokay geckos are largely insectivorous, pursuing their insect prey through a maze of branches and leafs. Captives can be fed crickets, grasshoppers and beetles. These should be dusted with mineral powders. Some geckos will also eat pinkie mice, which serve as a useful source of calcium. Because tokays will only eat prey that is alive and moving, frozen pinkies may have to be jiggled a bit to fool the lizard into eating them.

Breeding

Tokay geckos are not particularly difficult to breed in captivity. The eggs are laid in pairs, attached to a tree branch or to the sides of the cage. Once the female begins laying, she will produce a new clutch approximately every forty days. The eggs develop slowly and may take as long as six or seven months to hatch. Hatchling tokays are about five inches long and look just like small versions of adult lizards. They reach sexual maturity in about one year.

The powerful water monitor needs a large, strong cage. This is not a lizard for the uninitiated.

Water Monitor
(Varanus salvator)

Level: Advanced
Size: Extra Large
Habitat: Tropical, Semi-Aquatic

Biology

Also known as the Malaysian monitor, the water monitor is a large, aggressive lizard that is native to southeast Asia. As the name implies, it is found most often along riverbanks and lake shores. Adults can reach up to six feet in length. With their sharp claws and powerful tails, water monitors can be difficult to handle safely. They should only be kept by experienced herpers.

Housing

Housing for a water monitor must be strong and secure. Conditions must be warm and humid, and a water pan large enough for swimming is a necessity. Like all diurnal lizards, water monitors require a strong source of ultraviolet light.

Feeding

In the wild, water monitors feed on fish, shore birds and small mammals, which they capture near or in the water. They will also scavenge on carrion. Captives can be fed rodents or chickens.

Breeding

These lizards are not often bred in captivity. Up to twenty eggs are laid in cavities dug into the riverbank. The eggs hatch in two or three months, depending on the temperature. The hatchling monitors are covered with bright yellow spots.

CHAPTER 6

Snakes

There are about 2,700 species of snakes, which are classified along with the lizards in the superorder Squamata (meaning "scaled ones"). The snakes make up the order Serpentes.

Leptotyphlopids

There are about eighty species of thread snakes, which are found in hot, dry areas of Africa, Asia and Latin America. A few species of thread snake—including the Texas blind snake and the western blind snake—can be found in the southern parts of the United States.

These small snakes, about one and one-half feet long, are highly specialized burrowers and resemble large earthworms in appearance. The head is the same diameter as the neck, and the whole body is round and thin. The scales are thick and very smooth, giving the reptile a slimy appearance.

Not much is known about the lifestyle of these serpents. They are secretive burrowers and spend their whole lives underground. Because their jaws are small and cannot open widely, they are limited to small invertebrate prey. Most species feed on termites and other insects. The snakes grasp the insects on the soft

Pipe snakes are predominantly natives of Southeast Asia.

abdomen and use their short jaws to suck out the body contents before releasing the empty chitinous shell.

Typhlopids

The blind snakes are another group of small, primitive burrowing snakes. There are about 180 species in this family. The best-known is the Brahminy blind snake, which is unusual among snakes in its par-

The tiny Brahminy blind snake is one of the world's smallest snakes.

thenogenic reproduction strategy. The Brahminy is the only member of this family to be found in the United States; although it is native to southeast Asia, it has been widely introduced to non-native areas. Its habit of hiding in the soil of flowerpots has earned it the name "flowerpot snake." At slightly over five inches in length, the Brahminy blind snake is one of the smallest snakes in the world.

The blind snakes actually do have eyes, but they are small and covered with translucent scales. Very little is known of the biology of these secretive snakes. The primary food is ants, termites and other insects.

Anomalepids

This is a primitive group of snakes, consisting of four genera and about twenty species. All of them are found in Latin America. Although they are closely related to the blind and thread snakes, the anomalepids lack any trace of pelvic girdles and are thus evolutionarily more advanced than the other burrowing snakes. Almost nothing is known of their lifestyle or natural history.

Uropeltids

This group of primitive subterranean snakes, known as the shield tail snakes and the pipe snakes, contains about fifty species. The shield tail snakes, which make up the subfamily *Uropeltinae,* are found solely on the Indian subcontinent. Like the other burrowers, the skull is compact and solid, and the eyes are small and buried under translucent body scales.

The characteristic feature of the shield tails is the large circular patch of thickened skin at the end of the blunted tail. Presumably this is used to plug up the entrance of the snake's burrow to protect it from predators.

The shield tails vary in length from one to three feet. They feed largely on earthworms. They are unusual among the primitive snakes in giving live birth instead of laying eggs.

The pipe snakes, in the subfamily *Cylindropheinae,* are a small, primitive family consisting of less than a dozen species. Most are found in Southeast Asia. They were

The false coral snake protects itself by relying on its coloring—similar to that of the venomous coral snakes.

formerly classified in the aniliid family but have now been placed in the uropelts.

Almost nothing is known about the uropeltids' natural history.

Aniliids

The aniliid family is a primitive family that used to contain a number of species known as pipe snakes. Scientists have re-classed the pipe snakes as part of the uropeltid family, and the aniliids now consist of just a single species, the false coral snake (*Anilius scytale*) from Latin America. This snake has black and red bands on its back to mimic the venomous coral snakes.

This juvenile Arafura wart snake will never obtain the size of its cousin, the Javan wart snake.

Acrochordids

The acrochordids or wart snakes have only one genus with three species. All of these are found in southeast Asia and Australasia. The elephant's trunk snake or Javan wart snake (*Acrochordus javanicus*) is, at a length of eight feet, much larger than its cousins the Indian wart snake or file snake (*Acrochordus granulatus*) and the Arafura wart snake (*Acrochordus arafurae*). All three species are exclusively aquatic and feed almost solely on fish.

Xenopeltids

This family of snakes contains only one species, the sunbeam snake, which is native to Southeast Asia. This three-foot snake is similar in appearance to a small boid. The common name comes from the brilliant iridescence of its smoothly polished scales, which refract sunlight into a rainbow of shimmering colors as it moves.

Loxocemids

This is another single-species family, containing the Mexican burrowing snake (*Loxocemus bicolor*). This semi-burrowing specie is active only at night and little is known of its habits or natural history. It lays eggs and preys on eggs and small vertebrates.

Boids

The boid family, which includes all of the ninety-five or so living species of boas and pythons, is widely represented in the herpetoculture trade and contains some of the best-known and widely kept species of snakes. For the most part, boas are found in North and Latin America, while the pythons are found in Africa, Asia and Australia.

Biologically, the boids are among the most primitive of the living snakes. All boids retain the vestigial bones of their pelvic girdles, all that is left of the rear legs of their lizard ancestors. In the males, the single remaining rear toe is enlarged to form a claw or spur, which is used during the mating process to stimulate the female.

Boids also differ from the more advanced snakes by retaining a left lung which, although quite a bit smaller than the right, remains fully functional. The boids also have heavier skulls and less moveable bones than their more advanced cousins.

Bolyeriids

This small group was once classed with the boids but has now been given family status of its own. It differs from the boids by lacking any pelvic girdle and by possessing only one functional lung. The bolyeriids contain only two genera, each with a single species. Both are found only on Round Island, a tiny speck of land (less than one square mile) off the coast of Madagascar. The Round Island burrowing boa (*Bolyeria multicarinata*) and the Round Island boa (*Casarea dussumieri*) are both severely endangered and are protected under Appendix I of the CITES treaty.

Tropidopheids

This Latin American and Caribbean group of snakes, numbering about twenty species in four genera, was once classified with the boids. Known as wood snakes or West Indian boas, the tropidopheids are a little-known group of reptiles that are not often kept in captivity.

A Round Island boa kept at the Jersey Zoo in England.

Most are between one and three feet in length and most are terrestrial in habits. A few are arboreal and several species are semi-burrowers. For food, they kill small rodents and lizards by constriction.

Colubrids

The colubrid family contains many well-known and widely kept varieties of snake, classified into a number of subfamilies. It is by far the largest and most diverse of the snake families—of the 2,700 species of living snakes, about 2,000 are colubrids. The colubrids are a "taxonomic garbage can," and many of its members have been placed there simply because they don't seem to fit anywhere else. As our knowledge of the taxonomy and evolutionary history of snakes increases, the large colubrid family is likely to be broken into several smaller groups.

Elapids

The elapid family contains about 170 living species, including the well-known cobras as well as the closely related kraits, mambas, and coral snakes. All of the members of this family are venomous, and many species, including the cobras and kraits, have caused human fatalities. None of these snakes should ever be kept by any private collector. Elapids which have had their

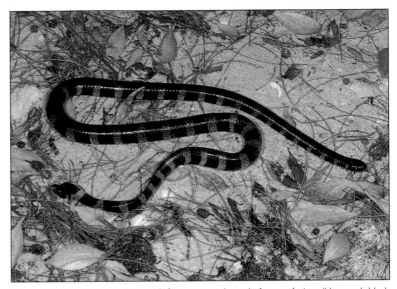

Sea snakes can remain submerged for over an hour before surfacing (blue and black sea snake).

venom glands surgically removed are occasionally available.

Hydrophiids

The fifty or so species of sea snakes are among the most highly specialized of the living reptiles. The sea snakes are so closely related to the cobras and kraits that some taxonomists prefer to place them as a subfamily of the elapid family. They have the same short, fixed fangs as their elapid relatives, but their bodies have been modified to adapt to a marine existence. Most species have tails that are laterally compressed, which helps them swim. A valve in the nose allows the snake to close its nostrils when submerged, and a special gland on the

head excretes excess salt from the body. They can remain submerged for over an hour before surfacing to breathe. Some sea snakes have a special light-sensitive detector on their tail, which tells them when a portion of their body is protruding from a burrow or shelter.

Atractaspidids

The "mole vipers" or "burrowing asps" have at various times been classified with the viperids and with the colubrids. Most taxonomists now classify them in their own separate family.

There are eight genera with fifty-five species, all of them venomous. Some genera have foldable fangs at the front of the mouth, while others have rear fangs like the colubrids. Most lay eggs, but a few species bear live young. Most feed on lizards and small rodents. One genus, Apparallactus, with eleven species, consists solely of specialized centipede-eaters. None of the mole vipers are widely kept as captives.

Viperids

As a whole, the viper family has a large number of members, about 180 species altogether. Only about fifty of these, however, are "true vipers," characterized by a lack of facial heat pits. Vipers are short, heavy-bodied snakes with broad heads—they are usually lethargic and nonaggressive unless disturbed. All of the vipers are venomous, and some have potent venom that has caused a large number of human deaths.

Although no true vipers are found in North or South America, they are widespread and common throughout Asia, Africa and Europe. The widest-ranging snake in the world, the European adder—found from the British Islands to the eastern areas of Russia and Siberia—is a member of the viper family.

Pit Vipers

The pit vipers are actually a subfamily of the viperids, known scientifically as the crotalines, consisting of about 150 species and making up the largest of the viper subfamilies. (Some taxonomists have argued in favor of separating the pit vipers into their own family, the crotalids). They are distinguished from the true vipers by the presence of heat-sensitive pits on either

side of the face. The familiar rattlesnakes are pit vipers, as are the North American copperheads and all of the Latin American vipers. With the exception of the coral snakes, which are elapids, the pit vipers are the only venomous snakes found in North America. Pit vipers are also common in southern Asia. They are not found in Africa.

Natural History

Snakes are the most recent of the reptiles to have evolved, but because their skeletons are delicate and do not fossilize easily, their early history is very poorly understood. The earliest snake to appear in the fossil record, called *Lapparentophis defrenni,* was found in the Sahara and dates to the early Cretaceous period about 130 million years ago, but it consists of only a few fossilized vertebrae. Recently another fossil, consisting of just two vertebrae, was found in Spain. The vertebrae are a few million years older than *Lapparentophis,* and this fossil has not yet been named.

The most complete skeleton of an early snake is known as *Dinilysia patagonica,* found in Upper Cretaceous deposits in Argentina. This six-foot skeleton has many characteristics similar to those of the modern boas and pythons, which are the most primitive of the living snakes.

European adders can be found from Britain to Siberia.

The earliest known fossil boid is *Madtsoia madagascarensis,* from the late Cretaceous period. The early boids were large, heavy-bodied snakes with a rather primitive and heavy skull structure. The living boas and pythons all have tiny clawlike toes protruding from either side of their cloaca. These are the remnants of the legs that their ancestors once had and are thus an evolutionary relic tying the snakes directly to their lizard ancestors. Some fossil pipe snakes have also been found from the late Cretaceous period in Wyoming and New Mexico.

Based on fossil finds, as well as on the anatomical study of modern reptiles, scientists have concluded that the snakes probably evolved from a family of lizards during the time of the dinosaurs. Snakes and lizards share a number of distinct features in the structure of their skull; both, for example, possess a moveable quadrate bone at the back of the jaw, and both are missing the quadratojugal bone at the rear of the skull.

One theory postulates that snakes are descendants of a family of lizards similar to modern-day monitors. These lizard ancestors, it is theorized, took to a burrowing existence, and as a result, they gradually lost their limbs, eyelids and external ears. Another theory postulates that snakes are the descendents of marine lizards, similar to the giant mosasaurs and that the loss of limbs, eyelids and ears is an adaptation to an aquatic existence. This theory was recently bolstered by the discovery of a fossil snake in Israel, known as *Pachyrachis,* which still possessed tiny rear legs and appears to have developed adaptations for swimming.

At an estimated length of fifty feet, the fossil snake *Gigantophis,* found in Egypt, was the largest of all the snakes.

Biology and Anatomy

Snakes and lizards are so similar in their anatomy that they are classified together in the same order of reptiles, the Squamata. In many ways, snakes can be viewed as elongated legless lizards. There are, however, several readily discernible differences between snakes and even the legless lizards. Unlike lizards, snakes do not have moveable eyelids. Instead, their eyes are covered by a transparent covering called a spectacle. Snakes also lack external ears or eardrums and are completely deaf to airborne sounds (although they are quite sensitive to vibrations). Snakes also possess a single row of large rectangular scales running along the belly, which are used in their unique methods of locomotion. Lizards, in contrast, always have a large number of very small ventral scales. Like lizards, though, snakes are ectotherms and cannot produce their own body heat. They can, however, tolerate a wider temperature range and are more widely distributed than their lizard cousins.

Heat Pits

Several families of snakes have developed sophisticated heat-sensitive facial pits to aid them in locating prey. In boas and pythons, these take the form of a row of pits in the upper lip; in the pit vipers, they consist of two openings on either side of the face. These structures are extremely sensitive to

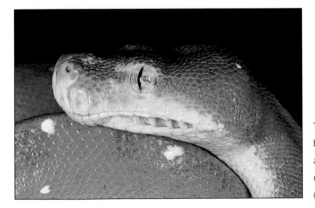

The heat pits of boas and pythons are located in a row in the upper lip (green tree python).

infrared radiation and can detect changes in temperature as small as one fourth of a degree Celsius. Snakes that possess these pits feed upon warm-blooded prey, sensing their presence by detecting their body heat. Blindfolded boas and pythons can locate and strike at prey using their facial pits.

Eyes

The anatomy of the snake's eye differs from that of any other vertebrate. All other vertebrates are able to focus a sharp image on the retina of their eyes by using special muscles to change the shape of the lens. Snakes lack these muscles and can only focus by moving the whole lens back and forth. As a result, the snake eye is not much more than a motion detector and is incapable of detecting details or stationary objects. Although they can tell the difference between light and dark colored objects, it is not clear whether snakes can actually see in color.

Jacobson's Organ

Because snakes have very poor eyesight, they depend largely upon their sensitivity to chemical signals to locate their prey and to find breeding partners. By continually flicking its long forked tongue, the snake picks up microscopic scent particles in the air and transfers them to the Jacobson's organ in the roof its mouth, which is rich in

chemical sensors. The Jacobson's organ is connected directly to the brain through the olfactory nerve. This chemical testing provides the snake with information regarding its surroundings. In this sense then, the snake "smells" with its tongue.

Skull

The snake skull has been heavily modified in response to its feeding habits. Snakes cannot chew, and they are therefore forced to swallow all of their food whole. To allow this, the bones of the snake's skull are loosely connected by flexible ligaments. The jaw joint can be dislocated to open the jaws to an extreme degree, and the two halves of the jawbone can also be spread widely apart at the chin. Snakes are thus capable of swallowing prey animals much larger than their own head. In venomous snakes, the teeth and skull have been further modified for the injection of venom.

Lungs

Like all of the paired internal organs, the lungs of a snake have been heavily modified to fit in a narrow elongated body. The right lung is large and extends for almost a third of the snake's length. Part of this lung encloses the lower part of the trachea, an extension known as the "tracheal lung." The left lung, in contrast, is greatly reduced in size and may be absent in some species. In effect, then, snakes have

only one lung. During feeding, when the mouth may be blocked for up to an hour, the snake extends its windpipe from the bottom of the mouth to breathe.

Heart

Snakes have the three-chambered heart that is typical of all herps. The blood is pumped to the lungs by one of the two atria and returns to the single ventricle, where it mixes with the oxygen-depleted blood that is returning from the rest of the body. It is then passed on to the other atrium to be pumped throughout the body. Because of this inefficient method of distributing oxygen, even the most active snakes tire easily and cannot sustain their activity for long periods of time without frequent stops to rest.

Skin

Snake skin consists of two layers. The inner layer contains the nerve endings and color pigment cells. The outer layer is made of keratin, the same protein from which human fingernails are made. The scales are made up of thickened portions of the outer layer. This layer is dead and cannot grow, and the snake must periodically shed it in order to increase its size. In this process of "ecdysis," the snake secretes a fluid between the two layers of skin and grows a new keratin layer underneath the old one.

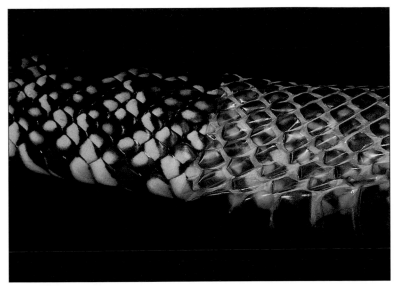

Snakes shed their outer layer of skin, usually in one large piece (Florida king snake shedding).

The old layer is then broken at the lips and is pulled off in one piece, inside out.

Stomach

Snakes use muscular contractions of the body to push food down the long esophagus into the stomach. The stomach can expand enormously to contain the large prey animals eaten by snakes. The digestive juices are powerful and nearly the entire prey animal is digested. The speed of digestion is dependent upon the temperature, and snakes that have just fed usually retreat to warm hiding places. A recently fed snake is vulnerable to predators, and if disturbed, it will often vomit. Food that took more than an hour to swallow can be regurgitated in just minutes.

Pelvic Girdle

Despite their lack of limbs, snakes can move quickly over a variety of terrains. Snakes do not actually walk on their ribs; instead, they use specialized sets of muscles attached to the rib cage to move the large ventral scales. Although the snakes' ancestors lost their limbs as an adaptation to burrowing, a few modern snakes still retain rudiments of their pelvic girdles, and members of the python and boa family retain a pair of external claws on either side of the cloaca—all that is left of their back legs. These claws are used in the mating process.

Hemipenes

All snakes practice internal fertilization, in which sperm are introduced directly into the female's cloaca. Male snakes possess a pair of copulatory organs called hemipenes, which are covered with a particular pattern of spines and knobs. During mating, only one of the pair of hemipenes is actually used; the arrangement of spines helps to lock it into place. Most snakes lay eggs, but a few species are ovoviviparous, meaning that the eggs are retained inside the female's body until they hatch, and the young are then born live.

In temperate areas, the sperm are produced during hibernation. In many species, if the male is kept artificially warm and not allowed to hibernate, the sperm will be killed by the abnormal heat, and the snake will not be capable of breeding.

Kidneys

Snakes have large, efficient kidneys that lie staggered in the snake's abdominal region with the left kidney located behind the right one. Like all reptiles, snakes are extremely efficient in their use of water. Most species can go without a drink for several months; several desert species never drink at all but obtain sufficient moisture from their prey. Mammals excrete nitrogen wastes in the form of water-soluble urea. In contrast, snakes excrete their wastes as crystals of uric acid, which form a dry white paste that is expelled along with the feces. Snakes thus have no urinary bladder.

Diseases

Anorexia

"Anorexia" is the medical term for refusing to eat—perhaps the single most common problem encountered by snake keepers.

Failure to eat does not mean that there is something wrong with your snake. Snakes normally go "off feed" for a period of several weeks prior to a shed. Males often refuse to eat during the breeding season, and females refuse food just prior to laying eggs or giving birth. Snakes from temperate regions will often go all winter without eating anything, even if they are kept warm and don't hibernate. Some species, such as ball pythons, are famous for going off feed for months at a time for no apparent reason, and then just as suddenly, they begin eating again. These fasts are not a problem as long as the snake is still active and is not visibly losing weight. Continue to offer food occasionally, and the snake will eat when it is hungry again.

Under other circumstances, refusal to eat is nearly always the result of some environmental problem. If your snake consistently refuses to eat, the first thing to check is the temperature in its cage. Probably three-fourths of anorexia cases are produced by temperatures which are too cool. The temperature in your snake's cage should be in the low 80s during the day, dropping to the mid-70s at night.

You should also ensure that your snake has a hide box available, because most snakes will not eat if they feel threatened or exposed to predators.

If your snake has a hide box, has suitable temperatures, has not shed its skin, and still has not eaten for more than six weeks, you should begin to suspect a medical problem. Refusal to eat is a symptom of a number of health ailments, including mouth rot and intestinal infections. You will have to take your snake to a veterinarian for a checkup.

Wounds

Wounds are most commonly seen in snakes that are housed with aggressive cagemates or that are being fed live food. Another common cause of wounds is rubbing the nose against the screen top in an attempt to escape, which may rub the scales raw and lead to infection. Snakes that are improperly housed can also suffer burns either from inadvertent contact with a basking light or from a malfunctioning hot rock or sizzle stone.

Smaller wounds and burns can be treated at home by applying an antibiotic ointment such as Neosporin, which is available at any drugstore, onto the injury. Snakes have a remarkable natural ability to heal wounds, and so long as the area is kept clean and disinfected with an antibiotic, it should

heal without further attention. If the wound is large or gaping, however, the services of a veterinarian may be needed to stitch it closed.

The best way to prevent burns and wounds is through proper housing. Aggressive snakes that are likely to bite one another should be housed separately. Hot rocks or sizzle stones should not be used, and basking lights must be carefully arranged so that the snake cannot reach them or physically touch them. One of the most common causes of wounded snakes is the practice of feeding live prey animals as food. All snakes should therefore be fed pre-killed prey exclusively.

Mouth Rot

Mouth rot, which is known under the technical name of infectious necrotic stomatitis, is a severe condition that is usually the result of an injury to the mouth, teeth or gums. Once the lining of the mouth has been broken by some minor injury, bacteria can invade the wound and multiply, where they produce a corrosive toxin that eats away the surrounding tissues. This produces a swollen red area inside the mouth that will continuously slough off dead tissues as well as a cheesy grey pus. The first sign is usually a refusal to eat, and examination of the inside of the mouth will reveal the telltale lesions and encrustation of dead tissue. If untreated, mouth rot will destroy the lining of the mouth and cause death.

You will need a veterinarian to attend to this problem. The doctor will swab the infected areas with a disinfectant like hydrogen peroxide and will also administer vitamin shots and antibiotics to help the snake fight off the infection. The sooner the condition is discovered, the better the chance of complete recovery.

Respiratory Infections

Respiratory infections are probably the most common cause of death among captive snakes. Infected snakes will begin having noticeable difficulty in breathing, and they may sneeze or make audible wheezing or bubbling sounds with each breath. Many times, the snake will breathe with its mouth held open. Fluid may leak or bubble from the nose. The snake may stop eating. If untreated, upper respiratory infections can spread to the lungs where they will produce pneumonia which is difficult to treat and will probably be fatal. Upper respiratory infections are highly contagious and can sweep quickly through an entire reptile collection, infecting nearly everybody.

This problem is the result of a bacterial infection, but it is nearly always brought on by keeping the snake at a temperature that is too low, leaving the snake's immune system too weak to fight off the invading bacteria. Tropical snakes are vulnerable to respiratory infections if they are chilled for even a short period of time. If it is caught early enough, the infection can usually be cured by improving the snake's conditions and raising the temperature to an acceptably high level (it may indeed help to keep the temperature a bit higher than normal until the infection clears up). Be sure to quarantine the snake until it is well.

If the condition doesn't clear up within a week or two or if it is so advanced that the snake breathes with its mouth open and is refusing to eat, you will need the help of a veterinarian. The vet will prescribe an injectable antibiotic such as tetracycline or baytril, and this will need to be injected every day for a period of several weeks. The vet will show you how to administer the injections and will supply you with the necessary drugs and syringes. Keep a close eye on the rest of your collection during this time.

After the infection has cleared, you will have to correct the environmental conditions that brought it on, or the infection is likely to return within a few weeks. The best preventive for respiratory infections is to maintain the proper temperature range and to carefully quarantine all incoming animals before any other snakes are exposed to them.

Intestinal Infections

The symptoms of an intestinal infection will be obvious and unmistakable. The snake will develop a severe case of diarrhea and will void watery, slimy feces that will have a powerful odor and may turn a greenish color. If it eats at all, it may shortly afterwards vomit up its meal. The culprit is a form of amoeba that attacks the intestinal linings. This is a serious disease that can kill a snake within a very short time. It is also highly contagious and can race rapidly through an entire collection of snakes, often with fatal results.

Contributory factors include temperatures that are too low and drinking water that is unsanitary and polluted with feces.

Treatment must be begun as early as possible. The veterinarian will start by administering doses of amoebicides such as Flagyl and may also provide fluids to fight dehydration.

Another common intestinal problem is the presence of worms or internal parasites. These cannot be detected by an external examination of the snake, but their presence can be indicated if the snake eats normally but never seems to gain weight—or actually becomes thinner. In very heavy infestations, there may be blood present in the feces, and if you examine an infected snake's feces, you may be able to see tiny threadlike worms present.

Worms are most common in wild-caught snakes.

If you suspect that your snake has worms, your veterinarian will need to see a recent fecal sample.

Inclusion Body Disease

Inclusion Body Disease is a very serious (but fortunately somewhat rare) disease that has only been recently discovered among captive snakes. Researchers at the University of Florida have isolated the virus that may be a causal agent of the disease and have been developing a blood test that may be able to provide a diagnosis, but testing so far has been inconclusive.

The disease is believed to be caused by a retrovirus and is invariably fatal (no cure or treatment is known). The disease seems to affect only members of the boid family, and although both boas and pythons are susceptible, boas are more likely than pythons to become "carriers" that harbor the virus but do not show any signs of infection.

The disease affects a variety of internal organs, including the kidneys, pancreas and spleen, but the most damage is done to the central nervous system, producing serious damage to the brain and spinal cord. Infected snakes therefore show bizarre neurological symptoms such as partial paralysis, inability to turn themselves over, and jerky or uncoordinated

motions. Many infected snakes develop a symptom known as "stargazing," in which the muscles of the neck involuntarily contract and pull the head upwards, until it looks as though the snake is looking at the sky. Sometimes the snake will actually raise itself up until it falls over backwards.

Other symptoms include vomiting and inability to swallow, and infected snakes often cannot shed their skin properly because they cannot control their bodies enough to peel off the old skin. Death comes from paralysis resulting in inability to eat or drink.

Inclusion Body Disease is highly contagious and appears to be spread through contact with exposed surfaces. The virus may also be spread by snake mites. Infected snakes may not begin to show symptoms until up to six months after exposure. Unfortunately, there is no known way to determine whether a living snake has the infection—the only conclusive diagnosis comes from a microscopic examination of the body tissues after death. The disease can therefore only be diagnosed in living snakes by the progressive appearance and worsening of the known symptoms.

Because there is no known cure or treatment for Inclusion Body Disease, it is recommended that any infected snakes be removed immediately and humanely euthanized.

Mites and Ticks

External parasites such as mites and ticks are probably the most commonly encountered health problem among captive snakes. The most obvious signs of infestation are a number of small moving dots on the snake's scales, particularly around the eyes and lips. These are snake mites, which are host-specific to snakes—your snake cannot get them from cats or dogs, only from other snakes or from contact with a surface containing mite eggs. Ticks are a bit larger and look like small black or brown seeds attached between the scales. Ticks are very common in wild-caught Latin American boids, such as boa constrictors and rainbow boas. They are also found fairly often in wild-caught reticulated pythons. Mites and ticks are both easily transmitted from one cage to another and may soon spread to infest your entire collection.

Both mites and ticks live by sucking blood from your snake, using their needle-like mouthpieces to pierce the thin skin between the scales. Although this loss of blood will not kill the snake by itself, it does weaken it to the point where it becomes vulnerable to other infections. Ticks and mites themselves can transmit a variety of disease organisms. They should be eliminated as soon as they are detected.

The best way to rid a cage of mites is to use a "no-pest" strip containing the insecticide Vapona. Such strips are readily available at most stores. Place a strip into a cloth bag, remove the water dish from the snake's cage and place the pest-bag inside for about three days. To kill any newly hatched eggs, this treatment should be repeated a week later.

Ticks are not as vulnerable to the insecticide as are mites, but fortunately tick infestations are not as common as mite infestations. The only way to ensure removal of ticks is to carefully examine the snake, scale by scale, searching for attached ticks. When one is discovered, it should be dabbed with a drop of alcohol to kill it, and then carefully removed with a pair of tweezers. Great care should be taken to avoid pulling the ticks out too roughly, as this may leave their heads and mouthparts still embedded under the snake's skin, where it can lead to an infection.

The best preventative for a mite or tick infestation is to carefully quarantine and examine any new arrivals.

Skin Problems

Most skin problems encountered in snakes will be the result of poor or incomplete shedding. The outer layer of a snake's skin is composed of the protein keratin, a dead biological material somewhat like plastic in its properties. This outer layer cannot grow, and therefore it must be periodically shed in order to allow the snake to get larger, a process called "ecdysis." Before shedding, the snake will usually stop eating and spend most of its time soaking in its water dish. About three weeks later, its skin will get noticeably darker, and its eyes will turn a hazy blue as the old outer layer of skin is separated from the inner layer. This blue color will disappear after a few days. About a week later, the snake will begin to retain fluids in its face, which causes the lips to swell and crack open the old layer of skin. The skin is then pulled off, inside out, in one continuous piece. Snakes will usually shed after having consumed between three and five meals.

Occasionally, snakes have trouble in attaining a complete shed. Boids in particular are prone to

If you discover a tick on your snake, dab the tick with a drop of alcohol to kill it, and then carefully remove it with a pair of tweezers.

peeling their skin off in large flakes instead of one complete piece, which often leaves pieces of old skin still attached. These are excellent breeding places for mites and certain bacteria. They can be removed by spraying the affected areas with a water mister or soaking the snake for several minutes in warm water, and then gently rubbing off the old skin. This problem usually indicates a humidity level that is too low, and it can be prevented by increasing the moisture content inside the cage. It may also mean that there aren't enough rough areas in the cage for the snake to hook its old skin and peel it off. To prevent this, snake cages should be provided with a pile of rocks and/or some gnarled branches for ease of shedding.

Although incomplete shedding is usually confined to boids, any snake can be affected by another fairly common shedding problem. Snakes lack eyelids and instead have a clear scale over the eye called the brille or eyecap. This is normally shed along with the rest of the skin during ecdysis. Occasionally, however, the eyecaps become detached from the rest of the skin and are not shed. Once the eyecap becomes detached in one shed, it tends to continue to remain in place during subsequent sheds. Eventually, these caps build up to the point where the snake can no longer see clearly, which can make it become defensive and irritable. They also serve as breeding grounds for bacteria and ectoparasites. For this reason, it is important to check the discarded skin after every shed to ensure that the eyecaps have come off and are not still attached to the eye.

If the eyecap is still attached, it can be removed by soaking the area with a damp cloth for a few minutes and then carefully lifting it off with a pair of tweezers. If there are several layers of shed built up over the eye, however, a veterinarian should address this problem, as improper removal can cause serious and permanent damage to the eyeball.

Captive snakes are also subject to a form of skin problem that has nothing to do with shedding. This is "blister disease," which takes the form of large fluid-filled blisters underneath the skin, particularly along the belly, which can burst open and become infected. It is most common in garter snakes and water snakes but is also seen in boids. Usually, blister disease is caused by environmental conditions that are too wet. Treatment consists of placing the snake in drier quarters. If necessary, your veterinarian can provide antiseptics to apply to the blistered areas.

Nutritional Problems

Snakes that are fed a diet of whole rodents, complete with viscera, bones and stomach contents, do not usually suffer from any nutritional deficiencies. However, water snakes are vulnerable to a Vitamin B deficiency that is brought about by a diet consisting solely of fish. This is caused by an enzyme in the fish, called thiaminase, that breaks down Vitamin B and makes it unusable by the snake. Advanced deprivation of Vitamin B causes tremors and convulsions in the affected snake and can cause death.

Treatment consists of vitamin injections that must be administered by a veterinarian. To help prevent this problem, water snakes should be given a variety of other prey in addition to fish, such as frogs and salamanders. Also, fish that are to be fed to water snakes should first be heated for three or four minutes at a temperature of around 150 degrees, which will destroy the thiaminase enzyme and allow the snake to utilize the fish's Vitamin B. The fish should be allowed to cool to room temperature before feeding to your snake.

Species Descriptions

Ball Python
(Python regius)

Level: Novice
Size: Large
Habitat: Tropical, Semi-Arboreal

Biology

Ball pythons are one of the smallest members of the python family, seldom reaching lengths of more than five feet. They are very heavy-bodied, however, and powerful for their small size. They are native to the central and western parts of Africa. In Europe, ball pythons are known as "royal pythons." When threatened, ball pythons will hide their heads inside the coils of their body and curl up into a ball, a habit that has earned them the nickname "shame snakes."

Ball pythons are very popular in the pet trade, and some 60,000 young snakes are sold in the United States each year. Unfortunately, most of these die in a short time from lack of proper care. If well-cared for, ball pythons can reach ages of almost thirty years.

A ball python will curl itself into a ball when threatened.

Housing

Ball pythons are not very active animals and spend most of their time curled up in a dark corner. A twenty-gallon aquarium is suitable space for an adult ball python. In the wild, they live in cavities in hollow trees and in captivity, they need a hide box to stay in, which they prefer to have off the ground.

They also need a relatively high humidity, particularly when they are getting ready to shed their skin. A large water dish will help to keep the humidity at acceptable levels as well as providing a place for the snake to soak. The air temperature should be kept at around 80 degrees with a hot spot for basking of approximately 90 degrees. Like most boids, ball pythons are crepuscular and are most active at dusk and dawn.

Feeding

In the wild, ball pythons eat a wide variety of prey animals, including rodents, small mammals, large lizards and birds. As mice and rats are not found in their natural habitat, wild-caught individuals often do not recognize these animals as food and refuse to eat them.

Captive-bred pythons are much easier to care for than wild-caught individuals, but even captive-bred ball pythons can be incredibly finicky eaters, sometimes refusing to eat for long lengths of time for no apparent reason. This is not dangerous as long as the snake retains its weight. Oftentimes, a ball python will gulp down a black rat after refusing white ones or will eat a bird after refusing rodents. Because of their finicky eating habits, wild-caught ball pythons are not recommended for beginning snake keepers.

Breeding

Although ball pythons are popular pets, they are rather difficult to breed in captivity, and most of the individuals in the pet trade are still imported. Male ball pythons can be distinguished from females by the claws on either side of the cloaca, which are longer in the male than in the female. During the mating ritual, these claws are used to stroke the sides of the female's body. There are some indications that ball pythons prefer to breed in groups with many males actively pursuing a single female.

Like all pythons, ball pythons are egg-layers with up to eight eggs per clutch. The female coils around these and protects them until they hatch, and during this period, she will not leave them to drink or eat. The eggs hatch in about ninety days, producing brightly colored juveniles that measure about one foot long.

If well fed, young ball pythons can grow as much as one foot per year, reaching sexual maturity in three or four years.

Black Rat Snake (Elaphe obsoleta)

Level: Novice
Size: Large
Habitat: Temperate, Semi-Arboreal

Biology

The black rat snake, which is closely related to the popular corn snake, is a large, active serpent native to the woodlands of the northeastern United States. At an average length of six feet and a maximum length of over eight feet, the black rat is the second longest snake in the United States; only the indigo snake grows longer.

Because of its shiny jet black skin, it is often referred to as the black snake. Another local name is the pilot snake, because of the mistaken belief that it always lives with, and serves as a lookout for, a

Black rat snakes will become docile captives over time (black rat snake with albino black rat snake).

rattlesnake. Although aggressive and defensive when first captured, black rat snakes soon calm down and become hardy and docile captives. They have lived up to twenty years in captivity.

Housing

Active and strong, black rat snakes require well-built escape-proof tanks. A twenty-gallon tank with a secure screen lid is a good home. Like all rat snakes, the black rat has sharp edges on the sides of its belly which help it keep a grip on bark and other rough surfaces, and this snake is an excellent climber. Captives should be provided with tree branches for climbing.

They are also good swimmers and will soak themselves in a water

dish for hours at a time. They can be kept on a bare pebble or gravel substrate, requiring only a hide box and a hot spot in one corner of the cage for basking.

Feeding

In the wild, black rat snakes eat rodents such as mice and small rats. They are also excellent climbers and will ascend bushes and trees to capture birds, nestlings and eggs. The eggs are swallowed whole, and the shell is then broken by contractions of the throat muscles. After the egg contents pass into the stomach, the broken shell is regurgitated.

Captive black rat snakes can be fed mice or small rats. A meal of one rodent every two weeks is sufficient. Pre-killed or thawed prey animals are always the best choice.

Breeding

As with most snakes, black rat snakes breed in the spring after emerging from hibernation. After a courtship ritual in which the female entices the male by rapidly vibrating her body, the female lays up to a dozen soft oval eggs in a hollow log or a shallow nest excavated in damp soil. Occasionally, several females will lay their eggs in the same spot.

The eggs hatch in about two and one-half months, producing brightly patterned twelve-inch hatchlings. The bold pattern fades with age, and adult snakes are plain black with a white chin. The young grow rapidly and reach sexual maturity in about two years.

Boa Constrictor
(Boa constrictor)

Level: Intermediate
Size: Large
Habitat: Tropical, Semi-Arboreal

Biology

This is perhaps the most famous snake in the world, but its popular reputation for size and aggressiveness is undeserved. There are six subspecies of boa constrictor found in Central and Latin America. All are considered endangered species, and most of the boas that are available in the United States have been captive-bred.

Boas are the second largest snake native to the western hemisphere, exceeded only by the anaconda, but they are dwarfed by the big Asian pythons. Typical boas reach about ten feet in length, although occasional specimens can get as long as fifteen feet. They are very hardy animals and are not difficult to keep. Captive boa constrictors have lived up to twenty-three years.

Housing

Boas are large, powerful snakes and require very spacious and strong housing. In the wild, they range from the dry deserts of Mexico to the wet rain forests of the Amazon Valley, and they can tolerate a wide range of environmental conditions. Temperatures in the 80s are best with a moderately high humidity. Boa constrictors are susceptible to respiratory infections if they are not kept warm enough.

Young boas are partly arboreal, spending a lot of time in trees, and they should be provided with vertical space and a number of tree branches to climb on. They are excellent swimmers, like to soak in water and must be provided with a water pool large enough to submerge themselves completely.

Feeding

Although boas will eat nearly anything they can capture, including birds, mammals and large lizards, rodents form the bulk of the diet. Newborn boas are large enough to swallow full-grown mice, and large individuals need to be fed chickens or rabbits. One good meal every two weeks is sufficient. If well fed, boas can grow amazingly quickly.

Breeding

Boas are not difficult to breed in captivity, and most of the animals available in the pet trade have been captive-bred. Female boas in the wild tend to breed only every other year. Breeding takes place at any time during the year, and the young are born live, approximately 100 to 150 days after mating. Litters range from twenty to fifty young, each measuring about one foot long. The

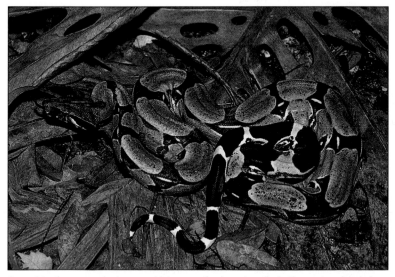

Second to the anaconda, boa constrictors are the largest snake in the western hemisphere (Peruvian redtail boa).

young grow quickly and reach sexual maturity in two or three years.

Bull Snake
(Pituophis sayi)

Level: Novice
Size: Large
Habitat: Desert, Terrestrial

Biology

Until recently, the bull snake was considered a western subspecies of the pine snake that had become adapted to a desert lifestyle. Today, it is classified as a separate species. In some parts of its range, it is known as the gopher snake. These are large and powerful snakes, reaching lengths of up to six feet.

In the wild, they are extremely defensive, and if cornered, they will rapidly vibrate the tip of the tail like a rattlesnake and may strike repeatedly. Like their cousins the pine snakes, bull snakes have a flap of skin in the throat that allows them to hiss very loudly as a threat gesture. Once captured, however, they tame quickly and make good captives.

Housing

Bull snakes are native to the dry, arid desert regions of the American West, and they prefer hot dry conditions. They do well in a large cage with a gravel substrate and a pile of rocks for hiding and climbing. The temperature should be kept at around 80 degrees with a basking light at one end to form a temperature gradient.

Although they are desert animals, they also need access to drinking water and will also soak occasionally. In the cooler parts of their range, bull snakes may hibernate during the winter and will sometimes stop eating even if their temperature is kept artificially high. If a captive bull snake stops eating during cool weather, it must be allowed to hibernate to prevent it from using up its fat reserves and starving.

Feeding

Like all snakes, bull snakes are entirely carnivorous and eat only animal prey. Smaller individuals will eat mice or birds, while larger specimens can consume medium-sized rats. A diet of one meal every two weeks is sufficient. Although some individuals may prefer to eat live prey animals, which they will kill by constriction, all snakes should be trained to eat pre-killed or frozen food as soon as possible. Bull snakes will oftentimes eat raw chicken eggs, which they will swallow whole.

Breeding

Bull snakes have a complex mating ritual that takes place in the spring. Rival males will sometimes engage in a "combat dance" with each male raising the front part of his body and trying to throw his opponent to the ground. During courtship, the males will often bite the female on the neck or back. About thirty days after mating, the female lays six to twelve large eggs which hatch in about two months. The hatchlings measure about eighteen inches in

When threatened, bull snakes will hiss loudly.

length and have bolder colors than their parents. These colors fade somewhat with age.

Burmese Python (Python molurus bivittata)

Level: Intermediate
Size: Extra Large
Habitat: Tropical, Semi-Arboreal/Semi-Aquatic

A Burmese python protecting a clutch of eggs.

Biology
The Burmese python is a subspecies of the Indian python, which ranges from Pakistan to the Pacific. The Burmese subspecies is found in the rain forests of southeast Asia, where it tends to stay close to populated areas. They are prized as food in many areas, and the Indian species is now listed as an endangered species.

The Burmese python is extremely popular in the pet trade, and thousands of hatchlings are sold in pet stores every year. Unfortunately, most people who buy them do so with no real idea of what lies ahead. The Burmese python is not a snake for a beginning herper. They are very large and powerful animals, and although they are not aggressive, they may be dangerous to handle alone. A typical Burmese python will reach twenty feet in length and weigh around 120 pounds. Occasionally individuals can reach twenty-five feet in length.

Because a captive python can live for over twenty years, caring for one of these animals is a lifelong commitment.

Housing
Burmese pythons grow quickly and require large strong cages. Young pythons are partly arboreal and need lots of vertical space with a number of tree branches for climbing. Older specimens stay on the ground.

Although they are very large, Burmese pythons are not active animals and will spend most of their time curled up in a comfortable spot. They need a moderately high humidity and temperatures in the 80s with a hot spot for basking. They also like to be near water and are never found far from it, so they will need a big pool in their cage.

Very large snakes can be given the free run of a room, as long as they are kept warm and provided with a pool for soaking and a spotlight for basking.

Feeding
Burmese pythons feed almost exclusively on warm-blooded prey. Juveniles feed largely on rodents and birds, while large adults are capable of killing and eating prey as large as goats and antelope. Very large specimens have been reported to have killed and eaten human beings, and several reptile keepers have been killed by these snakes.

Like all boids, the Burmese python is a constrictor, enveloping its prey in its coils to kill it. Contrary to popular belief, they do not crush their prey, but merely squeeze the chest cavity every time the prey exhales, until it can no longer breathe and suffocates. Captive Burmese pythons can be fed rats, while larger specimens will need a rabbit or chicken every week to keep them healthy.

Breeding
Like all boids, Burmese pythons are legally protected in the wild,

and nearly all of the snakes available in the pet trade have been captive-bred. Mating is usually triggered by a shortening of the daylight hours and thus usually takes place in the winter months. The female lays approximately forty-five eggs about two and one-half months after mating.

Like most pythons, the female Burmese provides a measure of parental care for her eggs and will coil around them protectively until they hatch. By using muscular contractions of her body, she is able to raise the temperature of the eggs above that of her surroundings and thus helps to incubate them. The young hatch in about two months and are then abandoned by their mother.

The hatchlings measure almost two feet long and can be fed mice and small birds. A well-fed Burmese python grows quickly, sometimes as much as three inches a month, and can reach a length of eight feet in just two years.

Corn Snake
(Elaphe guttata)

Level: Novice
Size: Large
Habitat: Tropical, Semi-Arboreal

Biology

The brightly colored corn snake is one of the most popular snakes in

Corn snakes are excellent climbers and should be provided with some vertical space and a number of branches.

the pet trade and is especially recommended for beginning herpers. The corn snake is a native of the southeastern United States and a member of the rat snake family, one of the few snake families to be found in Europe, Asia and North America.

The name "corn snake" is derived from the snake's boldly checkered belly scales, which resemble the Indian corn found at Halloween. Because of its bright, orangish coloration, the corn snake is also known as the red rat snake. Like all rat snakes, corn snakes are docile and hardy captives, reaching lengths of five to six feet. Captive corn snakes have lived for as long as twenty years.

Housing

Appropriate housing for the corn snake is representative of that required for any medium-sized temperate snake species. A fifteen-gallon aquarium can comfortably house a pair of snakes. As all snakes are superb escape artists, the tank must be provided with a tightly secured screen lid with a spotlight in one corner for basking. Newspaper makes a suitable (although unattractive) substrate. The snakes can also be kept on gravel or pine bark.

A hiding place must be provided where the snake can feel secure, either in the form of a rock cave, an overturned piece of bark or a hide box. This should be small enough that the snake can curl up in it while touching all four sides. A water dish must also be provided for drinking as well as soaking, and this should be large enough for the snake to submerge itself completely.

The water must be changed frequently because snakes often defecate in their water dish. Corn snakes are excellent climbers, and their cages should provide vertical space with a number of tree branches.

Feeding

In the wild, corn snakes eat small rodents, nestling birds and bird eggs. In captivity, juvenile corn snakes can be fed baby mice or small frogs such as tree frogs. Adults will eat mice.

As with all snakes, corn snakes should be fed pre-killed or frozen mice rather than live prey, as a live rodent is capable of severely injuring or even killing a snake. Adult corn snakes can be kept healthy on a diet of one mouse every two weeks. If whole prey is offered, no vitamin supplements or ultraviolet lights are necessary.

Breeding

Corn snakes are reliable breeders in captivity, and captive-bred hatchlings are readily available. Like most snakes, corn snakes breed in the spring. Captives must be allowed to hibernate before breeding season, because the male develops sperm only during cooler weather.

Approximately six weeks after mating, the female lays up to twenty eggs in a shallow nest. The eggs hatch in about seventy days, depending on the environmental conditions. In captivity, it is best to remove the eggs and incubate them manually. The method of incubating snake eggs is similar for most species. The best substrate for the eggs is a mixture of water and vermiculite, and they should be partially buried in this mixture. Turning the eggs over may injure the embryo inside, so they should be placed in the incubator in the same position as they were laid. The temperature should be maintained at about 85 degrees. The eggs also need to be kept damp while incubating and should be checked occasionally for signs of fungus infections. Wiping the eggs with a weak vinegar solution will help prevent mold and fungus attacks.

The hatchlings are brightly colored and boldly patterned, measuring about twelve inches long.

They reach sexual maturity in about three years.

DeKay's Snake (Storeria dekayi)

Level: Intermediate
Size: Small
Habitat: Temperate, Burrower

Biology

These diminutive little snakes are found in damp woodlands throughout the northeastern United States, but because they remain hidden most of the time, they are seldom seen, even in areas where they are common. Also known as northern brown snakes, they are often found in inhabited areas such as graveyards, city parks and vacant lots. DeKay's snakes rarely exceed two feet in length.

DeKay's snakes remain hidden most of the time and are rarely seen in the wild even though they often live in developed areas.

Housing

The DeKay's snake is an inhabitant of swamps and moist woodlands, and in captivity, it requires a damp substrate of moss or leaf litter. The substrate must be misted every morning. If the cage gets too dry, the DeKay's snake will die of dehydration, even if a water dish is provided. However, if the cage is kept too damp, it is vulnerable to blister disease.

A ten-gallon aquarium is sufficient space for this snake. A screen lid is necessary for ventilation, as the snakes cannot tolerate stagnant air. The tank must also have a shallow water dish for soaking and a number of hiding places in the form of rock caves or upturned pieces of bark. Although usually diurnal and active during the day, the DeKay's snake may become nocturnal during hot weather. Hibernation takes place in groups which congregate in underground burrows or fissures. Often, the snakes will gather inside ant hills for hibernation where they are protected from intruders by the ant colony. Captive DeKay's snakes can be kept active through the winter if maintained at suitable temperatures.

Feeding

In the wild, the DeKay's snake eats invertebrates that it finds among the leaf litter on the forest floor, including slugs and caterpillars. Captives do well on a diet of earthworms and salamanders.

Breeding

The DeKay's snake is not often bred in captivity. In the wild, mating takes place in the spring after the snakes emerge from hibernation. The male DeKay's snakes find the females by following their odor trail. The young are born live about three months later with an average litter size of around a dozen. The newborns measure just three or four inches in length.

Dumeril's Boa
(Boa dumerili)

Level: Intermediate
Size: Large
Habitat: Tropical, Semi-Arboreal

Biology

The Dumeril's boa was at one time classified in a separate genus, *Acrantophis,* but has now been placed with the Latin American boa constrictors. The Dumeril's, however, is an African snake found on the island of Madagascar. It is also sometimes referred to as the Madagascar ground boa.

A rather small boid, the Dumeril's boa reaches lengths of up to six feet. Because of habitat loss in its native island, the Dumeril's boa is listed as endangered, and its export is regulated. Nearly all of those available in the United States have been captive-bred.

Housing

Dumeril's boa is largely terrestrial in its habits, spending most of its time hidden among leaf litter on the forest floor. It does sometimes ascend into low trees or shrubs. It requires warm and humid

The Dumeril's boa is an endangered species—buyers should be certain that their boa was captive-bred.

conditions, similar to those needed for its Latin American cousins.

The Dumeril's boa is not often found far from water, and it should be provided with a large water pan in captivity.

Feeding

Like all boids, the main prey consists of warm-blooded animals such as birds or mammals. In captivity, rodents provide an acceptable diet.

Breeding

Dumeril's boas, like all boas, give live birth rather than laying eggs. Breeding takes place during the dry, summer months after the hibernation period. The courtship ritual consists of chin rubbing and prodding. The young are born live between six to eight months after breeding; they are about two feet long when born. Dumeril's boas have a life span of about twenty years.

Emerald Tree Boa
(Corallus caninus)

Level: Advanced
Size: Large
Habitat: Tropical, Arboreal

Biology

The emerald tree boa is an attractive species that is native to the rain forests of the Amazon River basin in Latin America. In appearance and habits, it is very similar to the

The large white patches on its back distinguishes the emerald tree boa from the green tree python.

green tree python, an unrelated species found in Australasia. In response to the pressures of a similar environment, both the emerald tree boa and the green tree python have evolved toward the same habits and body style, a phenomenon known to biologists as "convergent evolution." The emerald tree boa can be distinguished from the green tree python by the presence of large white splotches along its back.

Emerald tree boas are nocturnal and exclusively arboreal, spending their whole lives in the forest canopy. They spend most of their time draped over a branch in a characteristic pose. They reach lengths between four and six feet and can live as long as twenty-five years.

As captives, emerald tree boas are nervous and defensive, snapping aggressively at anything that approaches their perch. Because they can hang on with their prehensile tails and strike for long distances,

and because they usually coil themselves at eye height, great care must be taken when handling this species.

Housing

Emerald tree boas are not very active animals and do not require very large cages. They do, however, need vertical cages with plenty of branches for climbing. Most of these branches should be horizontal in orientation, so the boas can curl themselves on top. The snakes prefer smaller branches with a diameter of around one inch.

It is also advantageous to have removable branches, so that when the boa needs to be removed from its cage (for cleaning) the whole branch can be lifted out, eliminating the need to pry the snake from the branch.

The humidity must be kept high, but emerald tree boas cannot tolerate stagnant air, so the tank must be well ventilated. The cage must be misted every morning.

The temperature in the cage should be maintained in the low 80s with a basking spot of around 95 degrees.

Feeding

One would assume that the staple food of an arboreal snake would be birds, but in reality, birds comprise only a small part of the emerald tree boa's diet. Most of their food consists of arboreal mammals and rodents. Captives can be fed pre-killed mice or rats with an occasional chick or small bird. Feeding tongs should always be used, as the emerald tree boa has elongated teeth to pierce the skin and feathers of its prey, and can inflict a nasty bite.

Emerald boas are constrictors, and they will seize their prey and constrict it before swallowing it. Typically, the snake holds the dead prey in its coils and swallows it from the bottom up, allowing gravity to help force the food into its esophagus.

Breeding

Like all boas, the emerald tree boa is a livebearer and does not lay eggs. Females are generally larger and heavier than males, but usually probing is necessary to reliably sex this species. Breeding behavior is triggered in the wild by the arrival of the rainy season with accompanying changes in temperature and rainfall. In captivity, breeding can be stimulated by dropping the temperature to 68 to 70 degrees at night and increasing the simulated rainfall. It is also best to keep the sexes in separate cages until breeding time when they can be introduced just as the artificial environmental triggers are produced.

The young are born six to seven months after mating. About ten young are born with each litter. The newborn emerald tree boas are about one foot long. Unlike their parents, which are apple green in color, the newborns are bright red or yellow. These bright colors fade over time, and at the age of one year, the snake has the green pattern typical of adult snakes.

The young snakes require a somewhat higher humidity than adults and are also more delicate, requiring close watch over their housing temperatures.

Garter Snake (Thamnophis sirtalis)

Level: Novice
Size: Medium
Habitat: Temperate, Terrestrial

Biology

Garter snakes are the most widespread snake in North America and frequently the most common snake to be encountered in the wild, as they can live even within inhabited areas, such as parks, graveyards and vacant lots. They are also known as "garden snakes." There are over a dozen subspecies scattered across North America, all of them characterized by three bright stripes running longitudinally down the back and sides. In some subspecies, these stripes may be bright red or blue.

Garter snakes are small snakes, rarely exceeding four feet in length, but when cornered, they may put up quite a fight, biting repeatedly and voiding the contents of their scent glands. They settle down quickly, however, and become very tame, though difficult to handle because of their speed and activity. Because they are undemanding and easily kept, garter snakes are highly recommended for beginning reptile keepers.

Housing

Although they are small, garter snakes are very active and require lots of room for wandering. They can tolerate much cooler temperatures than most snakes—in the wild, they range up into Canada almost up to the Arctic Circle, but will normally hibernate when the temperature gets too low.

Garter snakes will thrive in a very simple cage with nothing more than a layer of gravel or newspaper as a substrate, a hot spot for basking and a hide box. They do not climb very often, but they do enter water readily and are very good swimmers. Great care should be taken to keep the cage completely dry except for the contents of the water dish, as garter snakes are very susceptible to fungal infections and skin blisters if they arc kept in conditions that are too damp. Captive garter snakes have lived over fifteen years.

Feeding

Garter snakes feed on a wide variety of prey animals, including small frogs, salamanders, earthworms, slugs and small fish. They are voracious feeders, and unlike most snakes, garter snakes may even accept food while they are getting ready to shed their skin.

Captives will do well on a diet of one or two goldfish per week, supplemented with an occasional earthworm. They can sometimes be taught to eat small strips of beef heart or liver, but whole prey animals are better from a nutritional point of view. Larger garters may accept baby mice. Garter snakes do not constrict their prey but simply seize it and swallow it alive. The saliva contains a mild venom which partially paralyzes the prey as it is being swallowed.

Breeding

Garter snakes are one of the easiest snakes to breed in captivity. In the wild, breeding takes place in the spring when the snakes emerge from hibernation. Each female may be pursued by several dozen males until one reaches the proper position for mating. After mating, part of the male's ejaculate will solidify and produce a temporary plug inside the female's cloaca, thus preventing any other males from mating with her. In cooler areas, the females usually breed only every other year.

In captivity, the female becomes most attractive to the male after she has shed her skin, and he will pursue her until she allows him to mate. The young are born live about 100 days after mating with anywhere from ten to seventy snakes per litter. Young garter snakes measure about six inches long when born but grow quickly, increasing their length by some 10 percent a month and reaching sexual maturity in about one and one-half years.

Green Snake (Opheodrys species)

Level: Intermediate
Size: Medium
Habitat: Savannah, Semi-Arboreal

Biology

There are two species of green snake native to the eastern part of the United States. The smooth green snake is found in the northern part of the country and measures about two feet long. The larger keeled or rough green snake grows to about four feet in length and is distinguished by the tiny ridges on its scales. Both species are a pale green color with whitish bellies, and this, along with their grassland habitat, has earned them the name "grass snakes." They are long, thin and very delicate snakes that are easily injured and should not be handled.

Green snakes do not adapt well to captivity and can be very difficult to keep successfully; they are nevertheless very common in the pet trade.

Housing

Both species of green snake are excellent climbers and require cages with lots of vertical space and plenty of tree branches and live plants. The smooth green snake is usually found in open grassy meadows, while the rough green snake is more arboreal.

Both species are diurnal and require bright lighting and a hot spot for basking. They cannot tolerate moisture, and their cages must be well-ventilated and kept dry except for the contents of their water dish. Both smooth and rough green snakes are excellent swimmers, and both may retreat to water if threatened, although they more often glide to safety among the branches of a low shrub.

Although they can be kept active throughout the winter if the temperature is kept artificially warm, they do better if allowed to hibernate. In the wild, they hibernate in communal groups in underground dens, often sharing a den with other snake species such as garter snakes.

Feeding

Green snakes are unusual among snakes in that they are entirely insectivorous, feeding on grasshoppers, caterpillars and spiders. Captives will survive on a diet of crickets, supplemented with soft-bodied caterpillars. However, they often refuse to feed in captivity and are not easy to maintain.

Breeding

Because they are difficult to maintain in captivity for any length of time, neither species of green snake is bred frequently. Males are usually shorter and somewhat thinner than the females. In both species, mating takes place in the spring. Smooth green snakes lay up to six eggs per clutch, oftentimes in a large communal nesting spot. The smooth green eggs are retained in the body until just before they are ready to hatch, and the young may emerge in as little as twenty days after the eggs are laid. The young are between four and eight inches long and capable of pursuing and catching small crickets and spiders on their own. The larger rough greens lay up to a dozen eggs, which will hatch in about twelve weeks.

The keeled green snake is more arboreal than the smooth green snake, but both snakes like to be surrounded by live plants and lots of branches.

Green Tree Python (Morelia viridis)

Level: Advanced
Size: Large
Habitat: Tropical, Arboreal

Biology

These beautiful snakes are native to northern Australia, New Guinea and the Solomon Islands. For a time, they were classified by themselves in the genus chondropython. Today, we know that they are closely related to the other Australasian pythons, and they are now classified together in the same genus.

Green tree pythons are exclusively arboreal and prowl among the tree branches in search of tree mammals and birds. In appearance and habits, they closely resemble the emerald tree boa of Latin America, which is also an arboreal hunter. This process, whereby two different animals come to resemble each other through similar environmental requirements, is known to biologists as "convergent evolution."

Although they are not very large, reaching adult lengths between five and six feet, green tree pythons can be nervous and aggressive as captives. Their long teeth are designed for penetrating the thick fur and feathers of prey animals, and they can give a nasty bite. Green tree pythons typically hang on branches at eye level with observers. This habit, combined with their ability to hang on with their tails and strike with almost the entire length of their body, makes them quite dangerous. Approach these snakes cautiously.

Housing

Green tree pythons are one of the smaller members of the python family. They tend to spend most of their time curled up on a tree branch in a characteristic resting position that makes them look somewhat like a bunch of unripe bananas. Because they are not very active, they do not require extensive cages. A tank with two feet on all sides and heavy branches for climbing is suitable for an adult python. Like all boids, they require tropical temperatures and high humidity.

Feeding

Although most of their food in the wild consists of birds and arboreal mammals such as bats, green tree pythons usually adapt to a diet of rodents in captivity. They prefer to hunt by hanging from a tree branch and lifting their prey into the air to constrict it. Usually, they will swallow their food upside down. Young green tree pythons will sometimes accept tree frogs.

Green tree pythons have been observed twitching the tips of their tails, apparently as a means to lure curious prey animals into striking range.

Due to their exceptional striking ability (and propensity), green tree pythons do not make good pets.

Breeding

Like all pythons, green tree pythons are egg layers. Between ten and twenty eggs are laid in a clutch, and these are brooded by the female until they hatch. The hatchlings are bright yellow or orange in color. This fades with age to the bright apple green typical of adults.

Hognose Snake (Heterodon species)

Level: Intermediate
Size: Medium
Habitat: Tropical, Terrestrial/Burrower

Biology

Hognose snakes can be immediately recognized by their distinctive, upturned snout, which looks like a pig's nose and helps the snake dig in the dirt for food. There are three species of hognose snakes found in North America. None are

very large snakes, and they seldom reach more than three feet in length. The eastern species is the largest, but the western is the most common in the pet trade.

Hognose snakes are famous for the bluffing act that they use to deter predators. When molested, the hognose snake will hiss and gape the jaws threateningly, and it can flatten the ribs behind its head to make its neck spread out somewhat like a cobra. Because of this elaborate threat display, the hognose snake is widely believed to be venomous and is known in many areas as the "spreading adder" or "puff adder."

If this bluff doesn't work, the snake will change its strategy and play dead; it will begin to writhe around as if in agony before rolling onto its back, holding the jaws agape and protruding its tongue. If it is rolled over onto its belly, it will promptly flip itself onto its back again.

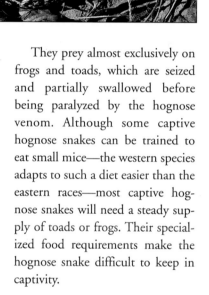

Hognose snakes are not dangerously venomous, although they will engage in the threatening behavior of a venomous snake to deter predators (eastern hognose snake).

Housing

In the wild, hognose snakes prefer dry woodland habitats and sandy, open scrub areas where they can find their favorite food—toads. They spend most of their time detecting hidden toads with their sensitive tongues and then digging them up with their upturned snouts.

In captivity, hognose snakes like a substrate that they can burrow in, such as dry soil or leaf litter. They are also somewhat shy and do best if they have a hide box where they can feel secure. They do not normally bask and do not need a hot spot.

Feeding

All hognose snakes have enlarged fanglike teeth in the rear of their jaws that can inject a mild venom to subdue their prey. However, they rarely bite, and the fangs are too far back in the mouth to be easily brought into play. Hognose snakes are not dangerous to people.

They prey almost exclusively on frogs and toads, which are seized and partially swallowed before being paralyzed by the hognose venom. Although some captive hognose snakes can be trained to eat small mice—the western species adapts to such a diet easier than the eastern races—most captive hognose snakes will need a steady supply of toads or frogs. Their specialized food requirements make the hognose snake difficult to keep in captivity.

Breeding

The eastern species of hognose snake rarely breeds in captivity, and most individuals of this species that are available are wild-caught. The western hognose snake has been successfully captive-bred and is becoming more readily available. The snakes mate in spring after emerging from hibernation, and the female lays a clutch of five to forty eggs in a patch of damp soil

or inside a hollow log in late June or early July. The eggs hatch in about two months. Hatchling hognose snakes measure about nine inches long and will perform the same threatening bluff as their parents. In captivity, they quickly become tame and will no longer perform their threat display.

King Snake
(Lampropeltus getula)

Level: Novice
Size: Medium
Habitat: Temperate, Terrestrial

Biology

There are nine subspecies of the common king snake in the United States. The most commonly encountered in the pet trade are the eastern or chain king snake, the California king snake, the Florida king snake and the speckled king snake. The rather rare grey banded king snake is a separate species. King snakes have a wide variety of colors and patterns, and even each subspecies may vary from striped to blotched to banded. All are cared for in the same manner.

King snakes are active and strong, reaching lengths of up to seven feet. When threatened, they may strike vigorously and expel musk from their anal glands, but they soon settle down and make good captives.

Housing

Large and active, king snakes require roomy cages with lots of hiding places. They are largely diurnal but may become nocturnal during hot weather. King snakes do not need much vertical room as they seldom climb and spend most of their time on the ground. A typical snake setup will do, including a gravel or newspaper substrate, a water dish, a hide box and a hot spot for basking. The air temperature should be in the low 80s with a basking spot of around 90 degrees.

In the wild, king snakes feed largely on other snakes. They must be housed individually, as they will eventually eat any tankmates, including other king snakes.

Feeding

Although they will eat rodents, lizards and sometimes birds, the major part of the king snake's diet consists of other snakes. They will even constrict and consume such venomous species as rattlesnakes, to which they are immune. By folding the prey in the stomach as it is being swallowed, a king snake can successfully eat even another snake that is longer than itself. In captivity, they will readily accept mice and other rodents.

Breeding

King snakes are not difficult to breed. However, the process must be watched closely, or one of the snakes may end up as a meal instead of a mate. Courtship consists of much writhing and twining, during which the male repeatedly bites the female on the back and neck.

The two-inch eggs are soft, oval and usually laid in early summer about forty days after mating. The clutch size varies from three to twenty-four eggs. The eggs hatch in about ten weeks, producing young snakes about ten inches long. The young may be highly variable in appearance, and in many subspecies, both banded and striped young will be produced from the same clutch. The young are ready to breed in about two years.

Milk Snake (Lampropeltus triangulum)

Level: Intermediate
Size: Medium
Habitat: Temperate to Tropical, Terrestrial

Biology

The milk snake is a member of the king snake family. It gets its name from its habit of prowling in barns and cow sheds in search of rodents, and also from the mistaken belief that it milks cows at night.

There are a large number of subspecies of milk snake, ranging from Canada all the way down to Latin America. Some of them, including the Sinaloan milk snake, have bright yellow, red and black bands around their bodies, which mimics the distinctive pattern of the venomous coral snake and gives the milk snake a measure of protection against predators. The common eastern milk snake is

This Florida king snake represents a new genetic strain developed in 1996.

The brightly colored bands of the Sinaloan milk snake resemble those of the venomous coral snake, helping to keep predators at bay.

patterned somewhat similarly to the copperhead. This pattern of imitation is known to biologists as "Batesian mimicry."

All of the milk snakes do well in captivity. They can live up to eighteen years and reach lengths of up to six and one-half feet.

Housing

As a group, the milk snakes inhabit a wide variety of habitats from dry, open fields to damp, tropical rain forests. The specific temperature and humidity requirements vary from subspecies to subspecies, but in general, temperatures in the 80s with a moderately high humidity are suitable. All of the milk snakes tend to be shy and retiring and need a hide box where they can feel secure.

Like their close relatives, the king snakes, milk snakes are confirmed snake-eaters and should not be housed with other snakes, even members of their own species.

Feeding

Milk snakes are eclectic feeders, preying on rodents, birds and their eggs, and other snakes, which they kill by constriction. Because they can fold the prey's body inside their stomachs, they can catch and consume even snakes that are much longer than themselves. In captivity,

they will thrive on a diet of mice or small rats, supplemented occasionally with a small bird egg.

Breeding

Although the common eastern milk snake from North America is hardy and makes a good pet, it is usually the more colorful races from Latin America, such as the Sinaloan milk snake or the Honduran milk snake, that are bred in captivity. In the northern races, breeding takes place in the spring after hibernation. Up to a dozen eggs are laid in early summer in a hollow log or patch of damp soil, and these hatch in about sixty-five days. Young milk snakes vary between six inches and one foot in length, depending on the subspecies. They can be fed baby mice

Milk snakes are constrictors and will consume other snakes even longer than themselves (Pueblan milk snake).

and small amphibians. They will also eat each other and should be separated after hatching. Milk snakes reach sexual maturity at about two years of age.

Racer
(Coluber constrictor)

Level: Intermediate
Size: Medium
Habitat: Savannah, Terrestrial

Biology
The racers are the only American species of a genus of snakes that is found largely in Europe. They are large and aggressive snakes that will often stand and fight if cornered, and they remain somewhat aggressive even after a long time in captivity.

As the name suggests, these are fast and active snakes that can move at almost four miles per hour—one of the fastest of the snakes. Racer snakes are unusual in having seventeen rows of scales at mid-body but only eleven or twelve rows near the tail. In addition, the skin of a racer is attached so tightly to the body that it cannot use its ventral scales to move in a straight line as other snakes can.

In some areas, the racer snake is known as the "hoop snake," because of the mistaken belief that it can take its tail in its mouth and roll along like a bicycle tire.

Contrary to popular belief, racers cannot roll along the ground like a tire—however, they do move very quickly.

Housing
Racer snakes are highly adaptable and can tolerate a wide range of environmental conditions. In the wild, they prefer dry, sandy scrub areas with scant vegetation. Although they are good climbers, they spend nearly all of their time on the ground.

Racer snakes can be kept in dry, warm cages with an air temperature of around 85 degrees and a basking spot in one corner. A large cage is required for these fast, active pets. Racers tend to be somewhat nervous and shy in captivity and will often refuse to eat unless provided with a hide box.

Feeding
The primary diet of racers consists of lizards, rodents and other snakes. They are diurnal hunters that use their great speed to run down their prey and capture it. Despite their scientific name, they are not constrictors—instead they use a loop of their body to hold down their prey while they swallow it. Captives can be fed pre-killed mice. They will also eat bird eggs on occasion.

Breeding
There are several varieties of racer found in the United States, all of which are part of the single species Coluber constrictor, and all of which can interbreed. The most common in the pet trade are the black racer and the blue racer.

In most racers, mating takes place in the spring after hibernation. The eggs are about one and one-half inch long and are laid in clutches of up to two dozen in damp soil or inside hollow logs. They hatch in about two months. The young snakes measure about ten inches long and are able immediately to fend for themselves. They reach sexual maturity in about three years.

Rainbow Boa
(Epicrates cenchria)

Level: Intermediate
Size: Large
Habitat: Tropical, Arboreal

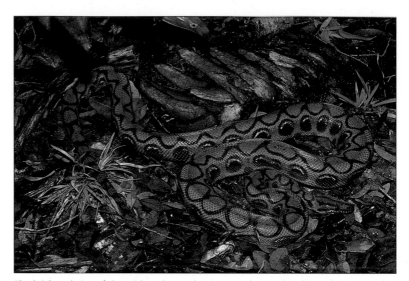

The bright coloring of the rainbow boa makes it a popular pet, but this snake is somewhat aggressive and will occasionally bite.

Biology

Rainbow boas are native to the rain forests of Latin America. They are spectacularly colored with brilliant shades of orange and red, and the scales produce an iridescent sheen, which gives these snakes their name. They are much in demand by collectors and can command a high price in the pet trade.

Rainbow boas are one of the smaller members of the boa family, seldom exceeding six feet in length. In care and habits, they are similar to the more common boa constrictor, but they tend to be a bit more prone to bite and become more aggressive as they get older. They can be kept tame, however, with regular handling.

Housing

Rainbow boas prefer habitats that are near water and seldom venture far from rivers or lakes. They are usually found at the forest edge near a body of water. Although rainbow boas have a prehensile tail and can climb well, they usually prefer to remain on the ground. The young tend to be more arboreal than the adults.

In captivity, they are not very active and do not require very large cages. The temperature should be kept in the 80s with a hot spot for basking, and a hide box should be provided. Rainbow boas require a very high humidity, however, of at least 80%, and this is best provided by placing a damp towel or moss in the snake's hide box. A large water dish will also keep the humidity high, as well as provide an opportunity for the snake to soak.

Feeding

In the wild, rainbow boas feed largely on birds and nestlings. In captivity, they will usually adjust to eating rodents. For adult boas, a diet of one medium-sized rat every two weeks is sufficient. Smaller snakes can be fed mice.

Breeding

Although these snakes are highly prized by collectors, not much effort is being made to captive-breed them. Rainbow boas exhibit typical boa breeding behavior. The male uses the small claws near his cloaca to stroke the female and stimulate her to breed. Up to a dozen young are born live about six months after mating. The young are about one foot long and have much brighter colors than their parents, whose colors fade somewhat with age. The Columbian species often loses its colors almost completely, fading to a dark chocolate brown color with age.

Reticulated Python (Python reticulatus)

Level: Advanced
Size: Extra Large
Habitat: Tropical, Semi-Arboreal/Semi-Aquatic

Biology
These huge snakes from southeast Asia, the largest snake in the world, can reach lengths of up to thirty feet and can weigh over 200 pounds. Although they adapt well to captivity and can live for over twenty years, they have a reputation for being aggressive and unpredictable, and zookeepers have been killed by reticulated pythons. They are not a snake for the inexperienced herper.

Housing
Although the reticulated python is a giant among snakes, it is not a very active animal and spends most of its time placidly curled up in a comfortable spot. In its native habitat, it may live near or even in inhabited areas. Because they are nocturnal and do not move around much, they are often never even seen by the villagers.

Juvenile captives can be kept in a large, well-built cage with vertical space for climbing and a hot spot for basking. In the wild, reticulated pythons do not usually stray far from water, and captives need to be provided with a water pool big enough to soak in. Retics grow quickly and will outgrow their tanks in little time. Large individuals can be given a room of their own, provided that they have a basking spot and a water pool available.

Although a big reticulated python will not usually resent such tasks as cage cleaning and maintenance, they are potentially dangerous animals and should never be handled alone.

Feeding
Reticulated pythons are powerful constrictors and have been known to kill and swallow animals as large

as a 100-pound leopard. There have also been documented cases of large retics eating human beings. Nearly any warm-blooded animal of manageable size will be taken. Captives can be fed warm-blooded prey that is appropriate for their size, ranging from mice for hatchling pythons to rats for juveniles, and continuing on to rabbits and chickens for adult specimens.

Breeding
Because of the large space required to breed reticulated pythons, they are not often bred outside of zoos, and most of the juveniles available in the pet trade have been imported. In the wild, reticulated pythons lay clutches of up to 100 large eggs, which are guarded and incubated by the female. The eggs hatch in about three months, producing

Reticulated pythons can constrict and consume large animals and have been known to even eat humans.

young reticulated pythons measuring about two feet long. The young reach sexual maturity at a size of about eight feet and an age of about three years.

Ribbon Snake
(Thamnophis sauritus)

Level: Novice
Size: Medium
Habitat: Temperate, Semi-Aquatic

Biology

Ribbon snakes look very much like garter snakes, to which they are closely related. They can be distinguished by the longitudinal stripes which lie along the second and third scale rows from the belly; in garter snakes, these stripes occupy the third and fourth row of scales. In addition, ribbon snakes usually have a recognizable yellow dot on the top of their heads.

There are several species of ribbon snake scattered throughout North America. They are nervous serpents and retreat rapidly if disturbed. Eastern ribbon snakes have been clocked traveling at over two miles per hour—pretty fast for a snake. They are also excellent swimmers and will often retreat into water, where they will swim away across the water surface rather than diving as do water snakes.

Ribbon snakes can grow up to three and one-half feet long, but they are very slender and can be easily injured.

Housing

In general, ribbon snakes prefer the same kinds of habitat as garter snakes, although they are much more aquatic than their garter snake cousins and are rarely found far from water. Ribbon snakes can be kept on a bare gravel substrate with a hide box and a large water dish. A hot spot should be provided in one corner. They can be kept successfully in the same tank with garter snakes. The entire cage must

Ribbon snakes prefer to eat fish and amphibians— this snake is enjoying a Cuban tree frog.

be kept dry, as ribbon snakes are very susceptible to fungal skin infections and blisters if their surroundings are too damp.

Feeding

In the wild, ribbon snakes and garter snakes are able to share the same habitat by dividing up the available food resources between them. The garter snakes feed largely on worms but will also eat slugs, salamanders and small fish. In contrast, the ribbon snake does not eat earthworms but concentrates on small fish and amphibians.

Captives will do well on a diet of two goldfish per week, supplemented occasionally by a salamander or small frog. Sometimes ribbon snakes can be taught to eat strips of fish, beef or liver, but these items should be no more than an occasional meal, as they do not contain the complete nutrition that whole prey animals provide.

Breeding

Breeding activities of ribbon snakes are similar to those of garter snakes. Mating usually occurs in the spring after hibernation with a large number of males pursuing each female. The young are born live, usually in late summer. The number of young per litter ranges from three to twenty-five, with an average litter size of about fifteen snakes. The newborn snakes are about seven inches long. If fed a diet of guppies, they grow quickly and reach sexual maturity in about two years.

Rosy Boa
(Lichanura trivirgata)

Level: Intermediate
Size: Medium
Habitat: Desert, Burrower

Biology

The rosy boa, also known as the California boa, is a small member of the boa family that can be found in hot arid areas from California and Arizona down to Mexico. It is one of the smaller snakes of the boa family, rarely exceeding three and one-half feet in length, and makes a docile and attractive pet. They are not a very common reptile, and there is concern that wild populations may have been affected by overcollection for the pet trade. In many areas, they are legally protected.

Not much is known about the rosy boa's habits or biology. It is known that they are largely nocturnal and often climb into shrubs or scrub in search of food. If threatened, they will curl themselves up and hide their head in their coils just like a ball python. Rosy boas are unusual among snakes in having two fully functional lungs. They have lived up to eighteen years in captivity.

Unlike most snakes, the rosy boa has two fully functional lungs.

Housing

In the wild, rosy boas prefer dry, arid hillsides with a scattering of vegetation. Captives need warm, dry cages with temperatures in the 80s and a hot spot for basking. A water dish for soaking and drinking is also necessary, and tree branches should be provided for climbing. Rosy boas tend to be shy and retiring and require several hide boxes to feel secure.

Feeding

Wild rosy boas eat rodents and nestling birds. Captives do well on a diet of one mouse per week.

Breeding

Rosy boas are not often bred in captivity, and most of the individuals that are available have been wild-caught. Like all boas, the rosy boa is a live-bearer. Mating takes place in the spring, and the litter of five to ten young are born about twelve weeks later. The newborn boas are relatively large (about twelve inches long) and are capable of eating small mice from birth.

Water Snake
(Nerodia species)

Level: Intermediate
Size: Medium
Habitat: Temperate, Semi-Aquatic

Biology

There are several species and over a dozen subspecies of water snake in the United States. At one time, they were all classified with the European water snakes in the genus *Natrix*. However, as all the American water snakes bear live young and all the Europeans lay eggs, the American species have been placed into the new genus *Nerodia*.

American water snakes can reach lengths of up to four feet. As the name suggests, they are never found far from water and drop into it at the slightest disturbance, diving to the bottom and hiding until the predator is gone. If captured, they are aggressive and pugnacious and will strike repeatedly while voiding the contents of their anal glands. As captives, water snakes are nervous and aggressive, usually biting with little provocation. A small number of people are sensitive to the mild anti-coagulant venom found in water snake saliva. They do not make good pets.

Housing

Because of their strong aquatic habits, water snakes require a large water pan in their tank, which should make up about half of the available space. The land area of the tank must be provided with a hide box and a hot spot for basking, and this must be kept completely dry. Water snakes are very prone to skin blisters and infections if they are not able to dry themselves off completely from time to time.

Feeding

In the wild, water snakes catch and eat a variety of aquatic vertebrates, including frogs, fish and salamanders. Captives can be fed a diet of whole fish, such as goldfish or minnows. Some water snakes can be taught to accept strips of fish or beef, but these foods lack a number of necessary nutrients. Whole prey animals are a better nutritional source. Captive water snakes are also prone to vitamin deficiencies if they are fed an exclusive diet of fish, and they should be fed prey animals such as frogs as a supplement.

Breeding

Like most snakes, water snakes tend to breed in the spring after emerging from hibernation. Often a mass of several dozen males will pursue each female. The young are born live about three months after mating with the litters averaging between ten and forty young. The newborn water snakes are about ten inches long and reach sexual maturity in about two years.

Yellow Rat Snake (Elaphe obsoleta quadrivittata)

Level: Intermediate
Size: Medium
Habitat: Tropical, Semi-Arboreal

Biology

The yellow rat snake is a large, active member of the rat snake group that is native to the southeastern United States. Their bright color pattern, yellowish-orange with four distinct black stripes running down the length of the body, makes them a visually intriguing pet. However, yellow rat snakes tend to be a bit more nervous than other rat snakes, and although not usually aggressive, they can be somewhat unpredictable in their

Water snakes are never found far from water (northern water snake).

temperament. Captive yellow rat snakes have lived up to twenty years.

Housing

Yellow rat snakes require housing typical of that for all rat snakes. They are semi-arboreal and readily ascend into trees in search of birds eggs and nestlings, and thus they need a tall enclosure with several branches for climbing.

Feeding

In the wild, yellow rat snakes eat rodents such as voles, mice and small rats, which they kill by constriction. They are also excellent climbers and will ascend trees to capture birds, nestlings and eggs. Captive yellow rat snakes can be fed mice or small rats. A meal of one rodent every two weeks is sufficient.

Breeding

Yellow rat snakes breed in the spring after emerging from hibernation. The courtship ritual is a long process, in which the female entices the male by rapidly vibrating her body. After much chin-rubbing, the male inserts one of his hemipenes into the female. The snakes may remain locked together for several hours. The clutch of twelve to twenty eggs hatch in about eight weeks, producing hatchlings with a blotched pattern on a dull grey background. As they grow, this pattern fades and is

Yellow rat snakes are climbers and should be provided with several branches for this purpose.

replaced by the adult yellow striped coloration. Like the other rat snakes, yellow rat snakes mature rapidly and can reach sexual maturity in about two years.

Venomous Snakes

Although it should go without saying that keeping venomous snakes (known as "hot" snakes) is very dangerous, both to oneself and to others, a number of venomous species, including such lethal serpents as cobras, vipers and rattlesnakes, are available from breeders and snake dealers. Most experienced snake keepers (including myself) would recommend that no one ever keep a venomous snake in a private home or apartment. In most areas, it is illegal to keep venomous species of snakes.

Keeping venomous snakes requires absolute concentration and attention that cannot waver for even an instant. Experienced

herpetologists and zookeepers with years of practice are bitten by venomous snakes every year, and very few people can go more than a few years actively handling venomous snakes without being bitten at least once. No one is immune to the single momentary lapse that leads to disaster. In fact, over half of all the snakebites reported in the U.S. are the result either of heroics in trying to capture or kill a snake found in the wild, or of accidents while handling a captive snake.

Snakebites are nothing to trifle with. Snake venom consists of a large number of components, nearly all of which are proteins manufactured in the snake's venom glands. Among the various types of proteins found in snake venom are proteolysins, which break down cell walls and destroy body tissues and blood vessels; hemorrhagins, which break open blood vessels and cause internal bleeding; cardiotoxins, which attack the muscles and nerve centers of the heart; and cytolysins, which attack and break down white blood cells.

The symptoms and effects of a hemotoxic snakebite will vary according to the size and species of the snake, the amount of venom actually injected, the location of the bite and the size and health of the person bitten. In general, though, the sequence goes something like this: Most bites occur on the fingers. At the instant of the bite, there is a sharp burning pain at the wound. Within one minute, the finger will be stiff and difficult to move, and discoloration will be noted at the bite site as the venom begins to break down body tissues and blood vessels. Within ten minutes, the whole finger will be black and discolored, and swelling will be noticeable. Within forty-five minutes, the swelling and discoloration will have reached the elbow. The pain by this point will be intense with severe throbbing and burning. Red streaks may be seen radiating away from the affected area as the venom continues to travel in the bloodstream. Over the next twenty-four hours, the entire limb will turn black and may swell to over twice its normal size. In some cases, the swelling may be so severe that the skin will burst open and produce large oozing sores. In serious bites, there may be a feeling of weakness and light-headedness, accompanied by a rapid pulse. Blood may drain from the nose, mouth or kidneys, and blood may also be vomited or passed from the intestines.

A severe bite may require treatment with as many as ten or twenty ampules of antivenin. Because each ampule may cost as much as $300 depending on the species (antivenin from foreign snakes will cost even more) and because the recovery process will necessitate several days in the hospital, a snake bite can be a very expensive as well as a very painful experience.

Other complications may arise. A proportion of people are allergic to horse serum and may develop an allergic reaction to the antivenin, experiencing anaphylactic shock, which is even more dangerous than the snakebite. Also, some people are allergic to the venom itself (and some people develop an allergy to snake venom after an initial exposure, making the second occurrence of snakebite far more dangerous than the first). In these cases, even exposure to the venom of a "mildly dangerous" snake can be quickly fatal.

Survivors of a snake bite may also undergo "serum sickness," which is a reaction to the antivenin used to treat the bite. This can produce severe flu-like symptoms with cramps, nausea and vomiting.

Whenever someone asks me about keeping a venomous snake, I always respond by telling the potential keeper to first obtain a large aggressive nonvenomous snake such as a water snake or coachwhip—something really mean and nasty—and keep it for a year. Feed it, change its water and clean its cage regularly. Every time the snake gets one of its teeth in you, write yourself a note saying, "I could be dead right now, and if I survived, I would owe the hospital $30,000 plus," and tape it to your snake cage. After a year, decide if you really want to keep a dangerously venomous snake.

Keeping venomous snakes demands the proper equipment. A snake hook is an absolute necessity for handling hot snakes. This is a long handle with a large metal hook at one end. When the hook is slid underneath the body of a viper or pit viper, the snake may be safely lifted and carried about. Because most vipers and pit vipers are heavy-bodied and lethargic, and because they are afraid of falling, they usually hang on tightly and make no attempt to get down or climb up the stick. Large snakes, such as gaboon vipers or diamondback rattlers, may need to be handled with two sticks. Because lifting a heavy-bodied snake on a hook may cause internal damage to the snake, it is safer to use the hook to "pull" the snake in a desired direction, more or less "herding" the animal into a bag or hide box.

One technique for handling venomous snakes is to pin the snake's head to the ground using a hook and then to grasp it with the hands just behind the jaws. This procedure is sometimes necessary for "milking" hot snakes of their venom for medical research. The amateur keeper, however, should have no reason to handle a snake in such a manner. Not only does it unnecessarily expose the keeper to the risk of a bite, but it can also damage the nerves and blood vessels of the snake's neck and even cause its death.

Fast and active snakes, such as cobras or mambas, will often refuse to stay "on stick" and will attempt to get to the floor or climb up the stick towards the handler. Using a snake hook on these species requires extensive training and great care. Another option is the use of "grab sticks," which are long tongs that close a pair of jaws around the snake's body when the handle is squeezed. These can cause severe injury to the snake, however.

The best method to handle aggressive venomous snakes is a "capture box." This is a hide box that has a clear glass door that can be slid over the entrance and locked into place, preventing the snake from leaving. Once the capture box is secured, the keeper can proceed to remove it and clean the rest of the cage.

If you absolutely must have a venomous snake (for use in educational exhibits and shows, for example) and have the proper training and experience to handle one, it is best to start with those species that do not have very powerful venom and normally do not threaten human life. These would include the copperhead, the European adder and the eyelash viper. Although bites from these serpents cause tremendous pain and tissue damage, they are not usually lethal.

Is there a way to keep a hot species of snake without all of these necessary legal and safety precautions? In many areas, "de-venomed" or "venomoid" snakes are available. These are venomous species, such as cobras, vipers and rattlesnakes, that have been surgically altered by a veterinarian, sometimes by removing the venom sacs completely using a laser, but more usually by making a small slit in the side of the snake's cheek and severing the duct leading from the snake's venom sac to the fang. This has the effect of rendering that particular snake incapable of injecting its venom.

A snake's venom is a part of its digestive process, and thus this process of de-venoming can have a serious impact on the snake's health. In general, vipers and pit vipers, which depend on their hemotoxic venom to break down body tissues for digestion, do not tolerate the operation very well, and most de-venomed viperids will stubbornly refuse to eat and die within months. Viperids in general also are more prone to stress than other snakes and do not tolerate captivity well—a condition that would only be aggravated by the stress of an operation. Although some viperids can be successfully de-venomed (usually long-term captives that have already become accustomed to eating pre-killed food), most cannot. The elapids, however, with their neurotoxic venom, seem better able to withstand the operation, and de-venomed cobras have been kept successfully in captivity for several years. The operation, again, is usually most successful in long-term captives that are already regularly feeding on pre-killed prey.

These "de-venomed" snakes are not able to inject any venom and thus do not present any danger of poisoning. However, although the venom ducts have been cut, the snake still possesses a full complement of fangs (the fangs cannot be permanently removed, because, like all of the snake's teeth, they are constantly replaced during life). This means that even though it may not be able to inject any venom, it can still bite and strike with its fangs, and such a bite can be extremely painful. It should also be pointed out that in a very few documented instances, snakes that had been de-venomed were able to recover their capacity to inject venom, either by regenerating a portion of their venom gland or because they possessed more than one duct. For this reason, even de-venomed snakes should be treated with respect and handled at all times as if they were hot.

It should also be noted that in some jurisdictions which have outlawed keeping venomous snakes, the fact that the snake is de-venomed may not change its legal status.

My own opinion is that the only justification for surgically altering a venomous snake is when the animal is to be used for educational purposes (lectures and talks), where safety considerations and insurance problems make using hot snakes impractical or undesirable. No snake should ever be surgically altered just to make a "pet" out of it. And it is my firm opinion that

A cape cobra from Africa spreading its hood.

no one should ever keep a venomous snake in a private home or apartment.

Nevertheless, a number of venomous species are available to experienced and properly trained amateur collectors. Many of these are also available as "de-venomed." The most commonly kept include the following:

Cobra
(Naja species)

Level: Experts only
Size: Large
Habitat: Tropical, Terrestrial

Biology

The cobra is perhaps the most famous and instantly recognizable snake on earth. The spreading hood is produced by elongated ribs in the snake's neck, which are erected whenever the snake is disturbed or angry. Cobras are nervous and defensive and strike repeatedly when threatened. Their aggressiveness, combined with their speed and agility, makes them extremely difficult to handle safely.

As a group, cobras range from Africa and across Asia. The most common species in captivity are the Egyptian cobra and the monacled cobra. Cobras were once considered to be fourteen separate subspecies scattered throughout Asia, but are now all classified as separate species.

The black necked cobra and the ringhals have modified fangs that allow them to eject a stream of venom for a considerable distance. Eye protection must always be worn when working with the "spitters."

Housing

The proper housing for captive cobras can be considered the standard for keeping any venomous snake. The cage must be sturdy and absolutely escape-proof. The best cages are molded from a single piece of plastic or fiberglass with sliding glass or plexiglass doors that can be secured with a padlock. The cage itself should be kept in a secure escape-proof room with a door that is kept locked at all times. If possible, the door should have a window to allow the cage to be viewed and inspected before anybody enters the room.

The cage furnishings should be as simple as possible to cut down on necessary maintenance and to make it easier to remove the snake if necessary. Most snakes require nothing more than a hide box and a water dish. The best hide boxes are equipped with a sliding glass or plexi-glass door that can be closed and locked while the snake is inside, allowing it to be safely removed for routine cage maintenance.

Feeding

In the wild, cobras eat a variety of foods, including other snakes. In captivity, they do well on a diet of mice or other small rodents.

Even venomous snakes should be fed pre-killed food to avoid danger to the snake. Prey animals should be offered with long-handled tongs or forceps.

Breeding

Cobras are unusual among snakes in forming monogamous pairs throughout the breeding season. The eggs are laid in a two-chambered nest with the eggs in the lower chamber and the parents guarding them from the upper chamber.

Copperhead
(Agkistrodon contortrix)

Level: Experts only
Size: Medium
Habitat: Temperate, Terrestrial

Biology

This small pit viper, reaching around three feet as an adult, is commonly seen in the eastern part of the United States. It spends most of its time hidden among dry, dead leaves on the floor of deciduous forests, camouflaged by its cryptic color pattern. The southern races are lighter in color and prefer a drier habitat.

Although the copperhead causes more venomous snake bites each year than any other species, it is not large enough to inject a lethal

Although the bite of a copperhead is rarely lethal, one should nonetheless use extreme caution with these snakes (broad banded copperhead).

dose, and deaths from its bite are extremely rare.

In the wild, most copperheads do not live longer than seven or eight years. Captives have lived as long as thirty years.

Housing

The copperhead is a lethargic animal and does not require a large cage. A small escape-proof enclosure with a hide box and water dish is suitable. It prefers temperate conditions with daytime highs in the upper 70s and nighttime lows in the low 70s. The copperhead will hibernate if conditions become too cool.

Feeding

In the wild, copperheads are eclectic feeders, preying on everything from frogs to lizards to large insects. Captives will usually eat small mice, which should be pre-killed and offered with long-handled tongs or forceps. Wild-caught northern

copperheads are usually stubborn eaters and will often refuse to eat until they starve themselves to death.

Breeding

Breeding takes place in the spring after the snakes emerge from hibernation. The young are born live with the litter size averaging no more than six young at a time. The young snakes have a bright yellow tip to their tail, which they use to lure frogs and large insects into striking range.

Eyelash Viper
(Bothriechis schlegeli)

Level: Experts only
Size: Small
Habitat: Tropical, Arboreal

Biology

These small, arboreal vipers are native to Central America. They are part of a group of snakes known

Projecting scales over the eyes give the eyelash viper its name (pink eyelash viper).

collectively as "palm vipers." The eyelash viper gets its name from the projecting scales over the eyes.

The species is found in several different color variations, including pink, green, and the highly prized yellow or "golden" race. Their small size (less than three feet) belies their ferocity and aggressiveness—they will gape threateningly at the slightest disturbance and will strike repeatedly at anything that approaches their perch. Although the snake is too small to inject a lethal dose, the venom is strong and can cause tremendous local tissue damage.

Housing

Eyelash vipers are exclusively arboreal and never descend to the ground. Their cage requires plenty of strong branches for climbing, as well as hot and humid conditions.

Feeding

Most of the eyelash viper's diet consists of small arboreal mammals, although it will also capture and eat birds. Usually the snake will strike

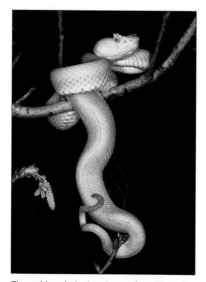

The gold eyelash viper is popular with snake enthusiasts and is widely bred in captivity.

its prey and hold on with the fangs until the venom has immobilized it. The prey is then swallowed upside down, using gravity to help force the food down the snake's throat.

Captive eyelash vipers can be fed pre-killed rodents, which should be offered on long-handled tongs or forceps.

Breeding

The eyelash viper (particularly the golden variety) is widely bred in captivity. The young are born live and are capable of fending for themselves from the moment of birth.

Gaboon Viper (Bitis gabonica)

Level: Experts only
Size: Large
Habitat: Tropical, Terrestrial

Biology

One of the largest vipers in the world, the gaboon viper can reach lengths of up to seven feet and is very heavy-bodied for its size. Its spectacular colors make it one of the most beautiful of the snakes, but its venom is lethal, making it one of the most dangerous snakes on earth.

The gaboon viper is native to the western part of central Africa where it lives in a tropical rain forest habitat. The gaudy color pattern helps to camouflage the snake while it lies half-buried in leaf litter, waiting for prey to wander by.

Housing

Gaboon vipers are lethargic and do not move around very much, preferring to spend most of their time curled up in their hide box. The cage requires nothing more than a suitable hide box and a shallow water dish. A temperature gradient of 80 degrees at the warm side and 75 at the cool end should be maintained. Gaboons live in deep forest and prefer subdued lighting. A basking light is not necessary.

Feeding

Gaboon vipers are ambush hunters that wait concealed on the forest floor until prey comes within range. They will eat everything from large amphibians to ground-dwelling birds, but the bulk of the diet is rodents and other mammals. In captivity, they will accept rats and rabbits.

One oddity about the gaboon viper is that it is sometimes incapable of finding its water dish and must be physically placed within it in order to drink every few days.

Breeding

Breeding this species is not difficult, and captive-bred gaboon vipers are widely available. Before breeding, the snakes should be given a "cooldown" period of about two weeks

With its highly toxic venom, the gaboon viper is one of the most dangerous snakes on earth.

at a temperature of 65 degrees. They should not be fed for several weeks beforehand.

After two weeks of cool-down, raise the temperature again and introduce the snakes to each other for two or three days before separating them for a day or two. This cycle can be repeated for up to four weeks.

The young are born live about six months after a successful mating. About two dozen young are born with each clutch. The young snakes are about one foot long. They are capable of striking and injecting venom from birth.

Pygmy Rattlesnake (Sistrurus miliarus barbouri)

Level: Experts only
Size: Small
Habitat: Temperate, Terrestrial

Biology

The pygmy rattlesnakes are found throughout the United States. The most common on dealers' lists, the Carolina pygmy rattler, is native to the southeast. As the name suggests, they are tiny serpents, seldom reaching three feet in length, with a rattle so faint it can hardly be heard at a distance. The rattles break easily, and wild specimens with intact rattles are rare.

The pygmy rattlers are faithful copies of their larger cousins, however, and will coil, rattle and strike just as the largest western diamondback when threatened. Although the venom is, drop for drop, one of the most powerful of the pit vipers, the tiny snake is not able to inject enough of it to be lethal, and deaths from these rattlers are virtually unknown.

One biological feature that differentiates the pygmy rattlers from their larger cousins is the head scalation. In the pygmy *Sistrurus* genus, the head scales are large and resemble those found on nonvenomous snakes. The *Crotalus* genus, which contains the larger rattlers, have heads covered in numerous small scales, like those of lizards.

Housing

Pygmy rattlers can be housed as any other venomous snake. Small escape-proof cages made of molded plastic are commercially available. These have sliding glass doors that can be secured with padlocks. Like most vipers and pit vipers, the pygmy rattlesnake stays "on stick" and is not terribly difficult to handle.

Feeding

The pygmy rattlesnake is an ambush hunter, curling up near a likely scent trail and waiting for potential prey to wander by. In the wild, they feed almost exclusively on lizards and frogs. Young snakes have also been observed feeding on large insects. There have been some reports of wild rattlers feeding on other snakes, including ribbon snakes. Wild snakes appear to use their tails as lures to entice frogs or other prey into striking range.

Captives will usually take small mice that are offered on long tongs or forceps.

Breeding

Like many snakes, male pygmy rattlers engage in ritualistic "combat dances" during the breeding season. Mating takes place in the fall, and the sperm are stored over the winter until April when the young begin to develop. Like most pit vipers, pygmy rattlers are live-bearers. Up to a dozen young are born in August. They remain with their mother for a few days until their first shed and then disperse. The female snake makes no effort to defend the young.

Western Diamondback Rattlesnake (Crotalus atrox)

Level: Experts only
Size: Large
Habitat: Desert, Terrestrial

Biology

One of the most widely known snakes in the world, the western diamondback has a reputation for fierceness. When threatened, it will pull itself into a striking coil, raise its head and neck into an **S**-shape and protrude the tongue vigorously. The venom is powerful, and the snake is large enough (it reaches lengths of up to seven feet) to inject a lethal amount of venom. This snake probably accounts for more lethal snakebites in the U.S. than any other species. In most areas, it is the most common rattler species to be found.

Housing

The diamondback is adapted to a desert existence and favors hot, dry areas with little cover. In captivity, they need temperatures in the 80s with a hide box to provide shade. Although large and bulky, they are not very active snakes and do not require very large cages.

The pygmy rattler has large scales on its head, similar to the scales of nonvenomous snakes (Carolina pygmy rattlesnake in red phase).

They are, however, very dangerous to handle, and snake hooks and capture boxes should be used at all times.

Feeding

In the wild, the primary prey of the western diamondback is rodents such as ground squirrels and prairie dogs. Captives will eat rats, rabbits or guinea pigs. Unlike some pit vipers, which refuse to eat in captivity, the western diamondback is not usually a finicky eater.

Breeding

These animals are regularly bred for the zoo trade and for research. The

The western diamondback rattlesnake has a lethal bite.

males track the females by scent, using their Jacobson's organ. When two breeding males meet, a "combat dance" occurs, in which both snakes intertwine their necks and try to force the other to the ground.

Like all rattlers, the young are born live. Litter size averages about twenty young, and the young rattlers are about one foot long.

On occasion, albino diamondbacks are available from breeders.

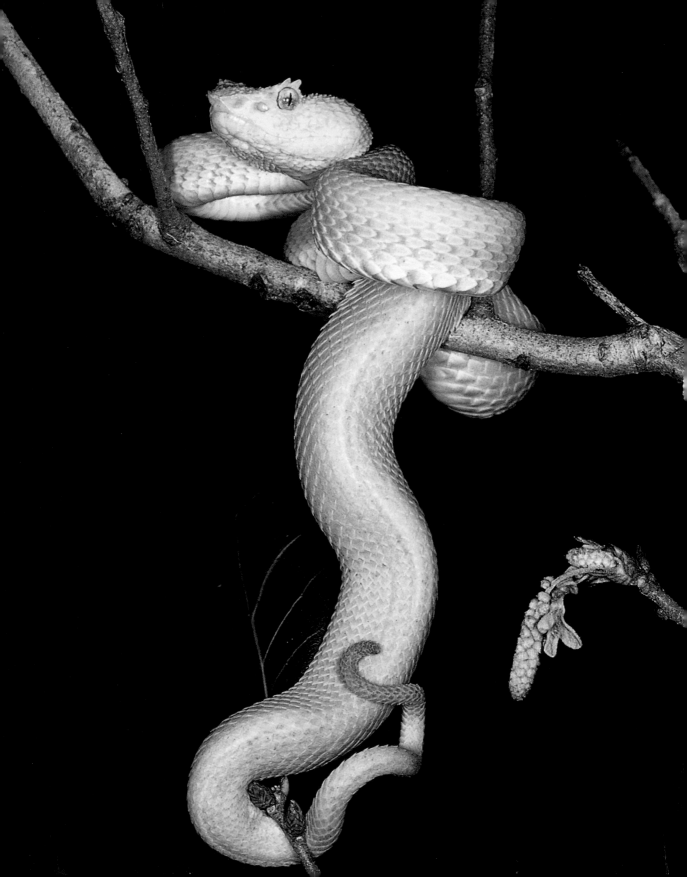

PART IV

Conservation of Reptiles and Amphibians

The Danger of Extinction

The Danger of Extinction

Unfortunately, many species of reptiles and amphibians are now becoming rare and are in danger of extinction, due largely to human activities. Many lizards, snakes and turtles, for example, are very popular as pets, and are now taken from the wild at increasing rates in order to feed the pet trade. Local populations cannot make up that kind of loss, and many species of reptile and amphibian are now under the protection of federal laws and international treaties concerning threatened and endangered species.

Habitat Loss

A far more devastating killer than the pet trade, however, is the loss of habitat and the fragmentation of existing range. Herp populations require a sizable contiguous area where they can forage for food and water. Housing developments and other construction projects, however, have fragmented most of the original habitats into small "islands" of wildland in a larger sea of cement and concrete. The tiny patches of undisturbed habitat that remain are not big enough to support a breeding population, and as a result, population levels of many American herps have dropped to dangerously low levels.

This steady loss of species can, in turn, have profound effects on the entire food web. The food web tends to be somewhat redundant; that is, certain species, if lost, can be readily replaced by other species that can fulfill the same ecological role. Today, however, humans are drastically reducing such large numbers of species that gaping holes are being ripped into the

local food webs, and we simply do not know enough yet about how all of these ecological chains are interconnected to foresee what kind of damage this will do.

It is for this reason that herpers must do all that we can to protect our natural resources and our natural biodiversity. By helping to educate others about the important ecological roles played by herps, and by taking steps to protect wild populations of reptiles and amphibians, we are helping to preserve and maintain the vast ecological web that supports all life on this planet—including us.

Fortunately, there are now a number of people fighting to preserve our reptile and amphibian biodiversity, along with the rest of our endangered ecosystems. And, because the pet trade has

traditionally been a primary offender in driving many species to the brink of extinction, it seems only fitting that today's responsible pet owners should have important roles to play in herp conservation. As a responsible herper, you too are part of a worldwide community that must involve itself in the protection and conservation of these creatures.

The Work of Herpetological Societies

The bulk of all herpetological education and conservation work in the United States is done, either directly or indirectly, by national, state and local herpetological societies. These are nonprofit organizations that are

Members of the Palm Beach Herpetological Society convene for an expedition.

formed by groups of private citizens, for the express purpose of furthering public education about reptiles and amphibians and promoting the conservation of wild herps. Herpetological societies also act to promote responsible keeping and captive breeding of reptiles and amphibians.

To help them meet these goals, herpetological societies carry out a number of tasks. Many herp societies carry out annual "field surveys," in which volunteer teams will comb wildlife habitats to take a census of the local reptile and amphibian populations. This allows researchers to study population trends of various species and may provide advance warning if populations of certain species are beginning to drop. It also helps state and federal officials monitor the populations of animals that are listed as threatened or endangered.

Herp society members also monitor local pet shops, ensuring that any reptiles and amphibians that are offered for sale are being kept in adequate conditions.

The most visible work of herpetological societies, however, is in the area of public education. Most herp societies sponsor talks and shows for the public where reptiles and amphibians are exhibited and people are educated about the vital roles that reptiles play in various ecosystems. Speakers are usually made available for school classrooms, Boy Scout troops and other groups or organizations that are interested in reptile and wildlife conservation. State and local herpetological societies may also provide witnesses and information for lawmakers and legislatures that are considering regulations and laws affecting reptiles and their keepers.

Herpetological societies work hard to ensure that all reptiles kept in captivity are done so safely, responsibly and in a way that does not endanger any wild populations.

Through newsletters, meetings, guest lecturers and other methods, herp societies disseminate a large amount of information and advice concerning the captive care and breeding of a wide variety of herps. Many local herp societies also work closely with local veterinarians and run "adoption" services that can provide good homes for herps that have been abandoned, confiscated or seized by local law enforcement or humane society officials, or simply given up for adoption.

I strongly encourage you to join your local herpetological society. Although membership in a herpetological society can cost between $15 and $35 per year, it is an investment that is well worth making for any herp enthusiast or hobbyist. Not only do you gain access to a rich source of experience and advice, but you will be helping to play an important role in maintaining and protecting these fascinating and unique creatures.

Resources

National Herpetological Societies and Associations

American Federation of Herpetoculturalists
P.O. Box 300067
Escondido, CA 92030-0067
(Publishes *The Vivarium*)

**American Society of Icthyologists
and Herpetologists**
Business Office
P.O. Box 1897
Lawrence, KA 66044-8897
(Publishes the quarterly journal *Copeia*)

National Herpetological Alliance
P.O. Box 5143
Chicago, IL 60680-5143

Society for the Study of Amphibians and Reptiles
Karen Toepfer
P.O. Box 626
Hays, KA 67601-0626

Amphibian Conservation and Research Center
1423 Alabama Street
Lafayette, IN 47905

International Society for the
Study of Dendrobatid Frogs
Ed Tunstall
2320 W. Palomino Drive
Chandler, AZ 85224

American Dendrobatid Group
Charles Powell
2932 Sunburst Drive
San Jose, CA 95111

International Venomous Snake Society
Thomas Marcellino
P.O. Box 4498
Apache Junction, AZ 85278

National Turtle and Tortoise Society
P.O. Box 66935
Phoenix, AZ 85082

International Iguana Society
Rt. 3, Box 328
Big Pine Key, FL 33043

International Gecko Society
P.O. Box 370423
San Diego, CA 92137

Local Herpetological Societies

(This listing is far from complete. If you contact the societies listed below,
they may be able to point you to a local herp society that is closer to you.)

Fairbanks Herpetocultural Society
Taryn Merdes
P.O. Box 71309
Fairbanks, AK 99707

Arizona Herpetological Association
P.O. Box 39127
Phoenix, AZ 85069-9127

Arkansas Herpetological Association
Glyn Turnipseed
418 N. Fairbanks
Russelville, AR 72801

Northern California Herpetological Society
P.O. Box 1363
Davis, CA 95616-1363

Southern California Herpetology Association
P.O. Box 2932
Sante Fe Springs, CA 90607

California Turtle and Tortoise Society
P.O. Box 7300
Van Nuys, CA 91409

Sacramento Turtle and Tortoise Club
Felice Road
25 Starlit Circle
Sacramento, CA 95831

San Diego Turtle and Tortoise Society
13963 Lyons Valley Road
Jamul, CA 92035

Colorado Herpetological Society
P.O. Box 15381
Denver, CO 80215

Southern New England Herpetological Association
470 Durham Road
Madison, CT 06443-2060

Delaware Herpetological Society
Ashland Nature Center
Brackenville and Barley Mill Road
Hockessin, DE 19707

Central Florida Herpetological Society
P.O. Box 3277
Winter Haven, FL 33881

West Florida Herpetological Society
3055 Panama Road
Pensacola, FL 32526

Turtle and Tortoise Club of Florida
P.O. Box 239
Sanford, FL 32772

Georgia Herpetological Society
Department of Herpetology, Atlanta Zoo
800 Cherokee Avenue SE
Atlanta, GA 30315

Idaho Herpetological Society
P.O. Box 6329
Boise, ID 83707

Central Illinois Herpetological Society
1125 W. Lake Avenue
Peoria, IL 61614

Hoosier Herpetological Society
P.O. Box 40544
Indianapolis, IN 46204

Iowa Herpetological Society
P.O. Box 166
Norwalk, IA 50211

Kansas Herpetological Society
Museum of Natural History, Dyche Hall
University of Kansas
Lawrence, KS 66045

Central Kentucky Herpetological Society
P.O. Box 12227
Lexington, KY 40581-2227

Louisiana Herpetological Society
Museum of Natural History
Foster Hall, LSU
Baton Rouge, LA 70803

Maryland Herpetological Society
Natural History Society
2643 N. Charles Street
Baltimore, MD 21218

New England Herpetological Society
P.O. Box 1082
Boston, MA 02103

Michigan Society of Herpetologists
321 W. Oakland
Lansing, MI 48906

Minnesota Herpetological Society
Bell Museum of Natural History
10 Church Street SE
Minneapolis, MN 55455-0104

Southern Mississippi Herpetological Society
P.O. Box 1685
Ocean Springs, MS 39564

St. Louis Herpetological Society
Harry Steinmann
P.O. Box 220153
Kirkwood, MO 63122

Northern Nevada Herpetological Society
Don Bloomer
P.O. Box 21282
Reno, NV 89502-1282

Association for the Conservation
of Turtles and Tortoises
RD 4, Box 368
Sussex, NJ 07461

New Mexico Herpetological Society
University of New Mexico
Department of Biology
Albuquerque, NM 87131

New York Herpetological Society
P.O. Box 1245
Grand Central Station
New York, NY 10163-1245

New York Turtle and Tortoise Society
P.O. Box 878
Orange, NJ 07051

North Carolina Herpetological Society
State Museum
P.O. Box 29555
Raleigh, NC 27626

Central Ohio Herpetological Society
217 E. New England Avenue
Worthington, OH 43085

Northern Ohio Association of Herpetologists
Department of Biology
Case Western Reserve University
Cleveland, OH 44106

Oklahoma Herpetological Society
Tulsa Chapter
5701 E. 36th Street N.
Tulsa, OK 74115

Oklahoma Herpetological Society
Oklahoma City Chapter
Oklahoma Zoo
2101 NE 50th
Oklahoma City, OK 73111

Oregon Herpetological Society
WISTEC
P.O. Box 1518
Eugene, OR 97440

Lehigh Valley Herpetological Society
Rich Rosevear
P.O. Box 9171
Allentown, PA 18105-9171

Philadelphia Herpetological Society
Mark Miller
P.O. Box 52261
Philadelphia, PA 19115

Pittsburgh Herpetological Society
Pittsburgh Zoo
1 Hill Road
Pittsburgh, PA 15206

Rhode Island Herpetological Association
30 Metropolitan Road
Providence, RI 02909

South Carolina Herpetological Society
James L. Knight
P.O. Box 100107
Columbia, SC 29230

Texas Herpetological Society
Hutchinson Hall of Science
31st at Canton
Lubbock, TX 79410

Utah Herpetological Society
Hogle Zoo
P.O. Box 8475
Salt Lake City, UT 84108

Washington Herpetological Society
12420 Rock Ridge Road
Herndon, VA 22070

Pacific Northwest Herpetological Society
P.O. Box 70231
Bellevue, WA 98008

Wisconsin Herpetological Society
P.O. Box 366
Germantown, WI 53022

Breeders and Dealers

Blue Chameleon Ventures
P.O. Box 643
Alva, FL 33920

Glades Herp, Inc
P.O. Box 50911
Fort Myers, FL 33905

Recommended Reading

General Reptiles and Amphibians

Behler, John and F. Wayne King. *The Audubon Society Field Guide to North American Reptiles and Amphibians.* New York: Alfred A. Knopf Publishing, 1979.

Conant, Roger. *A Field Guide to Reptiles and Amphibians of Eastern and Central North America.* Boston: Houghton-Mifflin, 1975.

Mattison, Chris. *The Care of Reptiles and Amphibians in Captivity.* London: Blandford, 1992.

Rosenfeld, Arthur. *Exotic Pets.* New York: Simon & Schuster, Inc., 1987.

Staniszewski, Marc. *Amphibians in Captivity.* Neptune City, NJ: TFH Publications, 1995.

Stebbins, R.C. *A Field Guide to Western Reptiles and Amphibians.* Boston: Houghton-Mifflin, 1966.

Frogs and Toads

Grenard, Steve. *Frogs and Toads: An Owner's Guide to a Happy, Healthy Pet.* New York: Howell Book House, 1998.

Heselhaus, Ralf. *Poison Arrow Frogs: Their Natural History and Care in Captivity.* Sanibel, FL: Ralph Curtis Books, 1992.

Mara, William. *Breeding and Keeping Frogs and Toads.* Neptune City, NJ: TFH Publications, 1994.

Salamanders

Bjorn, Byron. *Salamanders and Newts: A Complete Introduction.* Neptune City, NJ: TFH Publications, 1994.

Indiviglio, Frank. *Newts and Salamanders: A Complete Pet Owner's Manual.* Hauppauge, NY: Barron's Educational Series, Inc., 1997.

Turtles

Bartlett, Richard D. and Patricia Bartlett. *Turtles and Tortoises: A Complete Pet Owner's Manual.* Hauppauge, NY: Barron's Educational Series, Inc., 1996.

Flank, Lenny Jr. *The Turtle: An Owner's Guide to a Happy, Healthy Pet.* New York: Howell Book House, 1997.

Obst, Fritz Jurgen. *Turtles, Tortoises and Terrapins.* New York: St. Martin's Press, 1986.

Lizards

Balsai, Mike. *The General Care and Maintenance of Savannah Monitors.* Lakeside, CA: Advanced Vivarium Systems, 1992.

Bartlett, Richard D. and Patricia Bartlett. *Monitors, Tegus and Related Lizards: A Complete Pet Owner's Manual.* Hauppauge, NY: Barron's Educational Series, Inc., 1996.

Grenard, Steve. *The Lizard: An Owner's Guide to a Happy, Healthy Pet.* New York: Howell Book House, 1997.

Hatfield, James W. *Green Iguana: The Ultimate Owner's Manual.* Portland, OR: Dunthorpe Press, 1996.

Rosenthal, Karen. *The Iguana: An Owner's Guide to a Happy, Healthy Pet.* New York: Howell Book House, 1996.

Snakes

Flank, Lenny Jr. *Snakes: Their Care and Keeping.* New York: Howell Book House, 1998.

Flank, Lenny Jr. *The Snake: An Owner's Guide to a Happy, Healthy Pet.* New York: Howell Book House, 1996.

Greene, Harry W. *Snakes: The Evolution of Mystery in Nature.* Berkeley, CA: University of California Press, 1997.

Kauffield, Charles. *Snakes: The Keeper and the Kept.* Malabar, FL: Krieger Publishing, 1995.

Mattison, Chris. *Keeping and Breeding Snakes.* London: Blandford, 1988.

Mattison, Chris. *The Encyclopedia of Snakes.* New York: Facts on File, Inc., 1995.

Ross, Richard. *The Reproductive Husbandry of Boas and Pythons.* New York: Institute of Herpetological Research, 1990.

Index

Note: Photographs of a particular animal are represented by italicized page numbers.